## OPPOSING VIEWPOINTS® SERIES

# Family

# Other Books of Related Interest:

## Opposing Viewpoints Series
Adoption
Male/Female Roles
Working Women

## At Issue Series
Do Children Have Rights?
Gay and Lesbian Families

# "Congress shall make no law . . . abridging the freedom of speech, or of the press."

*First Amendment to the U.S. Constitution*

The basic foundation of our democracy is the First Amendment guarantee of freedom of expression. The Opposing Viewpoints series is dedicated to the concept of this basic freedom and the idea that it is more important to practice it than to enshrine it.

# OPPOSING VIEWPOINTS® SERIES

# Family

*Karen Miller, Book Editor*

**GREENHAVEN PRESS**

*An imprint of Thomson Gale, a part of The Thomson Corporation*

I.C.C. LIBRARY

THOMSON

━━━━━✦━━━━━ ™

GALE

Detroit • New York • San Francisco • New Haven, Conn. • Waterville, Maine • London

Christine Nasso, *Publisher*
Elizabeth Des Chenes, *Managing Editor*

© 2008 The Gale Group.

Star logo is a trademark and Gale and Greenhaven Press are registered trademarks used
herein under license.

*For more information, contact:*
Greenhaven Press
27500 Drake Rd.
Farmington Hills, MI 48331-3535
Or you can visit our Internet site at http://www.gale.com

LIBRARY OF CONGRESS CATALOGING-IN-PUBLICATION DATA

Family / Karen Miller, book editor.
    p. cm. -- Opposing Viewpoints
    Includes bibliographical references and index.
    ISBN-13: 978-0-7377-3741-7 (hardcover)
    ISBN-13: 978-0-7377-3742-4 (pbk.)
    1. Family--United States. 2. Family policy--United States. I. Miller, Karen.
    HQ536.F33817 2008
    306.85--dc22
                                                                    2007030794

ISBN-10: 0-7377-3741-7
ISBN-10: 0-7377-3742-5

Printed in the United States of America
10 9 8 7 6 5 4 3 2 1

# Contents

## Chapter 3: How Does Divorce Affect Children?

## Chapter 4: Should Government Make Policies Regarding Families?

# Why Consider Opposing Viewpoints?

*"The only way in which a human being can make some approach to knowing the whole of a subject is by hearing what can be said about it by persons of every variety of opinion and studying all modes in which it can be looked at by every character of mind. No wise man ever acquired his wisdom in any mode but this."*

*John Stuart Mill*

In our media-intensive culture it is not difficult to find differing opinions. Thousands of newspapers and magazines and dozens of radio and television talk shows resound with differing points of view. The difficulty lies in deciding which opinion to agree with and which "experts" seem the most credible. The more inundated we become with differing opinions and claims, the more essential it is to hone critical reading and thinking skills to evaluate these ideas. Opposing Viewpoints books address this problem directly by presenting stimulating debates that can be used to enhance and teach these skills. The varied opinions contained in each book examine many different aspects of a single issue. While examining these conveniently edited opposing views, readers can develop critical thinking skills such as the ability to compare and contrast authors' credibility, facts, argumentation styles, use of persuasive techniques, and other stylistic tools. In short, the Opposing Viewpoints series is an ideal way to attain the higher-level thinking and reading skills so essential in a culture of diverse and contradictory opinions.

In addition to providing a tool for critical thinking, Opposing Viewpoints books challenge readers to question their own strongly held opinions and assumptions. Most people form their opinions on the basis of upbringing, peer pressure, and personal, cultural, or professional bias. By reading carefully balanced opposing views, readers must directly confront new ideas as well as the opinions of those with whom they disagree. This is not to simplistically argue that everyone who reads opposing views will—or should—change his or her opinion. Instead, the series enhances readers' understanding of their own views by encouraging confrontation with opposing ideas. Careful examination of others' views can lead to the readers' understanding of the logical inconsistencies in their own opinions, perspective on why they hold an opinion, and the consideration of the possibility that their opinion requires further evaluation.

## Evaluating Other Opinions

To ensure that this type of examination occurs, Opposing Viewpoints books present all types of opinions. Prominent spokespeople on different sides of each issue as well as well-known professionals from many disciplines challenge the reader. An additional goal of the series is to provide a forum for other, less-known, or even unpopular viewpoints. The opinion of an ordinary person who has had to make the decision to cut off life support from a terminally ill relative, for example, may be just as valuable and provide just as much insight as a medical ethicist's professional opinion. The editors have two additional purposes in including these less-known views. One, the editors encourage readers to respect others' opinions—even when not enhanced by professional credibility. It is only by reading or listening to and objectively evaluating others' ideas that one can determine whether they are worthy of consideration. Two, the inclusion of such viewpoints encourages the important critical thinking skill of objectively evaluating an author's credentials and bias. This evaluation will illuminate an author's reasons for taking a particular stance on an issue and will aid in readers' evaluation of the author's ideas.

It is our hope that these books will give readers a deeper understanding of the issues debated and an appreciation of the complexity of even seemingly simple issues when good and honest people disagree. This awareness is particularly important in a democratic society such as ours in which people enter into public debate to determine the common good. Those with whom one disagrees should not be regarded as enemies but rather as people whose views deserve careful examination and may shed light on one's own.

Thomas Jefferson once said that "difference of opinion leads to inquiry, and inquiry to truth." Jefferson, a broadly educated man, argued that "if a nation expects to be ignorant and free . . . it expects what never was and never will be." As individuals and as a nation, it is imperative that we consider the opinions of others and examine them with skill and discernment. The Opposing Viewpoints series is intended to help readers achieve this goal.

*David L. Bender and Bruno Leone,*
*Founders*

# Introduction

*"Public concern over changes in the practice of marriage is approaching hysteria. An avalanche of books and articles declares that the American family is in a severe state of crisis. Yet little agreement exists among experts on what the crisis is about, why it has occurred, or what could be done. . . . The current situation falls somewhere between those who embrace the changes with complete sanguinity and an increasingly vocal group who see the meltdown of the so-called traditional family as an unmitigated disaster."*

—Frank F. Furstenberg Jr.,
*professor of sociology
at the University of Pennsylvania*

"Family" is a word that conjures up images of home, security, safety, and love. Everyone is born into a family; Hollywood gives us scenes of octogenarians dying peacefully, surrounded by loved ones. For good or ill, it is the one institution all humans have in common. So why is it such a source of controversy? Politicians and social commentators have engaged the nation in a heated conversation about "family values" and the definition of family, and proponents on all sides of the topic are riled up.

This debate over family and its place in society is nothing new. In his essay, "The Future of Marriage," Frank Furstenberg Jr. remarks that the current idealized definition of the "traditional" family—a heterosexual married couple and their children—itself represents a mid-twentieth century divergence from the then-traditional portrait of family as an extended, multigenerational kinship group living closely together. During the 1950s, sociologists expressed anxiety about whether such a small family unit could survive the enormous pressures that isolation would place on a married couple when they had only each other to turn to for companionship and support. In the first chapter of the book *Reinventing the Family*, author Elisabeth Beck-Gernsheim describes the diversity of family even earlier in history. Eighteenth-century church registers show that stepfamilies were common, with men and women marrying several times over the course of their lives. Men of the ruling classes had wives and mistresses and acknowledged illegitimate offspring with positions and titles of their own. Laws often restricted access to marriage among the working and peasant classes; unmarried men and women united and raised children together anyway.

But if the "traditional" family has always been just one arrangement among many, why is the current dialogue about its latest transformations so virulent? It is insufficient to say that people fear change and cling to what they know. Society changes, and individuals work to maintain their beliefs during changing times. In the late twentieth century and early 2000s, however, technology completely transformed how people interact with others and how they conduct their lives. From making it easier to work from home to finding personalized medical treatments and to organizing like-minded people around the globe, technology has made the modern world much more one of individuals. In this world of individuals, people seek individualized forms of expression and association that are frequently at variance with how things used to be done.

Stepfamilies have occurred for hundreds, if not thousands of years, but historically mostly people were free to remarry only when their spouses died. By contrast, in the late 1900s and early 2000s spouses can dissolve marital relationships and try marriage again. Children acquire stepparents when their biological parents are still alive. Ex-spouses wonder how to maintain relationships with former in-laws. Such situations are common and often times difficult to manage.

Moreover, improvements in transportation and communication have made it easier for people to relocate. Families frequently move to pursue professional opportunities. Although they can stay in touch with friends and relatives they leave behind, the dislocation of individuals across nations and continents means that friends and relatives are no longer immediately on hand to look after children, to assist with household projects, or provide companionship. As Jane Lewis points out in *Should We Worry about Family Change?*, governments suddenly have to decide if they value their adult citizens more as workers who can contribute to national growth or as parents who raise children to perpetuate national culture and values. Should public funds be spent to help parents work less and educate their children more or to help parents work more by paying for their children's childcare?

Perhaps the most significant impact technology has had on family and society has been to separate sex and procreation from marriage. Contraception methods reduced the risk of pregnancy from extramarital sex, and when pregnancy out of wedlock occurred there was less community objection or sense of shame. As the shame disappeared, more people openly conducted sexual relationships without getting married and then started raising children in those unmarried relationships. Social attitudes about out-of-wedlock births have generally become more permissive. Assisted reproductive technology first enabled infertile married couples to conceive and bear their own children and then enabled single women to conceive and bear children with anonymous sperm donations. Homosexual couples used donated sperm and eggs and the wombs of surrogate mothers to conceive and bear their own children. Older single women used donated sperm and eggs to bear children that were genetically unrelated to them. Children are adopted across international borders. Previously, biology was inextricably tied to parenthood. Today, it is not required that a man and woman—much less a married man and woman—combine to make a family. Many different combinations of adults and children are describing themselves as family in contrast to the traditional definition of that word.

Family formation is truly in flux. Some people relish the possibility of change, and others seek safety in habit and custom. Because the course of their lives is influenced by their own families, those in which they are born and those they create for ourselves, people feel strongly about the social practices and formal policies that arise concerning family issues. The four chapters of *Opposing Viewpoints: The Family*—What Are Some Characteristics of the Modern Family? What Dilemmas Do Would-Be Parents Face? How Does Divorce Affect Children? and Should Government Make Policies Regarding Families?—examine some of the factors directing the debate about family, from the personal to the national level. The discussion really is an important one because its subject affects everyone, one way or another.

# CHAPTER 1

# What Are Some Characteristics of the Modern Family?

# Chapter Preface

To some extent, families are unchanged across time and cultures. Children are born to adults who take care of them by cooperatively providing their physical necessities and teaching them how to be members of their society. These children, in turn, become adults responsible for creating and rearing the next generation. But in many ways, "family" as practiced in modern times is quite different from its historical counterpart. Multigenerational households, patriarchal leaders, proximity of siblings, and vast networks of cousins are rapidly vanishing.

The modern family, particularly the modern American family, exists in a highly individualistic culture. Ever since thirteen colonies severed their ties to the "mother country" of England during the American Revolution, citizens of the United States have been striving to live up to an ideal of independence and self-governance and making their own marks upon the world. In 1739, in *Poor Richard's Almanack*, Ben Franklin wrote: "Let our Fathers and Grandfathers be valued for their Goodness, ourselves for our own." One hundred years later, Ralph Waldo Emerson penned his famous essay, "Self-Reliance," in which he espoused the idea that "the great man is he who in the midst of the crowd keeps with perfect sweetness the independence of solitude." In 1902, suffragette Elizabeth Cady Stanton made the plea for women's rights and freedom and "the solitude and personal responsibility of her own individual life." Echoes of this call to women resurfaced in 1964, with the publication of *The Feminine Mystique* by Betty Friedan: "The only way for a woman, as for a man, to find herself, to know herself as a person, is by creative work of her own. There is no other way."

The suggestion that people have responsibility to themselves and their personal fulfillment is quite different from

Old World (European) values. The creation of the self-reliant citizen in the eighteenth and nineteenth centuries contrasts sharply with the codes of family loyalty and allegiance. The plays of William Shakespeare, written between the years of 1590 and 1613, illustrate the dynamic of how the needs of the family superseded the needs of the individual; they do so most famously in *Romeo and Juliet,* when two young lovers from feuding families kill themselves rather than be separated.

Modern values of individualism and self-actualization appear to conflict with the values regarding forming a family and raising children. How can one live for one's own self and still take on the responsibility of others? Much of the current debate about family in a culture of individualism involves drawing lines between the (seemingly conflicting) rights of parents and children. Are the rights of one person, regardless of age, more important than another? Does the pursuit of individual desires negatively affect the structure of a home? Are families more vulnerable if they are not surrounded by kin? The authors in the following chapter explore the bonds of love, obligation, and society that surround the modern family and judge to what extent the individuals that compose a modern family should pursue their separate rights to liberty and happiness.

*"In historical perspective, the breadwinner-housewife type of family most people in the West define as tra-ditional is actually an uncommon ar-rangement."*

# Traditional Families Never Were "Traditional"

## Arlene Skolnick

*Arlene Skolnick is a faculty member of the Institute of Human Development at the University of California, Berkeley. The following viewpoint explains how economic factors, mortality rates, and fertility rates have affected the structure of the family throughout history and in the modern era. In this viewpoint, the author argues that there is no decline of the "traditional family" because the "traditional family" never really existed.*

As you read, consider the following questions:

1. When did the concept of the traditional family—headed by a breadwinner and housewife—first emerge?
2. How have lower fertility rates changed the marital rela-tionship?

Arlene Skolnick, "The Triple Revolution: Social Sources of Family Change," *The Family on the Threshold of the 21st Century*, Danvers, MA: Erlbaum, 1997, pp. 167–80. Copyright © 1997 by Lawrence Erlbaum Associates, Inc. Republished with permission of Lawrence Erlbaum Associates, Inc.

3. How have the reduction of infant mortality and the increase of life span affected the state of the family?

Over the past three decades [from 1967 to 1997], family life in the industrialized nations changed dramatically. The trends are remarkably similar across North America and Western Europe: a divorce revolution, a sexual revolution, couples marrying later, a drop in fertility rates, an increase in single-parent families, an increase in the number of women working outside the home, and an increase in the diversity of family forms. As a result of these and other changes, there is also increasing uncertainty about how to define the family, and widespread concern over whether the institution will continue. . . .

Although it is obvious that a major transformation occurred, there is no consensus as to what it means. Is the family a disappearing institution? Have individuals in recent years become more self-centered, less willing to make commitments or to invest in family ties? Whereas scholars debate whether or not the family is in decline, or merely changing, the general public, particularly in the United States, assume the disintegration of the family to be a simple social fact, part of a general breakdown of morals and values. These anxieties have made family issues a major battleground in American politics.

## "Family" in Crisis throughout History

There have been relatively few efforts to make sociological sense of the recent upheavals in family life, or to place them in historical context. Social analysis often consists merely of noting demographic trends, such as rising divorce rates or rates of unwed motherhood and making attributions about the individual motives and values that might account for them. In fact, however, as the burgeoning field of social history shows, family life has always been in flux. At periods of societal transition, change is especially rapid and dislocating. . . .

The era we are living through today bears many resemblances to two earlier periods of family crisis and transformation in Western history. The first is the time of transition when the preindustrial family-based economy began to give way to the urban, industrial way of life, with its separation of work and family. In the United States, this shift began in the early decades of the 19th century.

Briefly, the movement of fathers and work out of the home disrupted existing patterns of daily family life as well as cultural blueprints for gender and generational roles. These dislocations in the functions and meaning of family life unleashed a wrenching era of personal stress, social disorder, cultural confusion, and political ferment. The crisis was eventually resolved when a new paradigm of family emerged that rationalized and sanctified the new patterns and practices.

No longer a workplace, the home as an emotional and spiritual refuge, a "haven in a heartless world," was at the center of the new model of family. And at the center of the home was the wife and mother, who would nurture both children and the father who had to enter the heartless world each day.

## Traditional Families: More Ideal than Real

The "new domesticity," with its doctrine of separate spheres for men and women, was a middle class creation, but it became the dominant cultural definition of *family* as well as a blueprint for the good and proper way to live. Few families could live up to the ideal in all its particulars; working class, Black, and ethnic families, for example, could not get by without the economic contributions of wives, mothers, and daughters. And even for middle class families, the sentimentalized Victorian image of family life prescribed a standard of perfection that was virtually impossible to fulfill. Nevertheless, the new model supplied the cultural coherence that had been sorely lacking; at last people had a definition of family not based on the household as an economic enterprise in which the family worked together.

Eventually, however, social change overtook the new domesticity. Around the turn of the 20th century, another period of rapid economic, social, and cultural change destabilized Victorian family patterns, especially its gender arrangements. Several generations of "new women" challenged the constraints imposed on women by Victorian domesticity. This ferment culminated in the victory of the woman's suffrage movement, the first wave of women's liberation. It was followed by the 1920s jazz age era of flappers and flaming youth, the first, and probably the major sexual revolution of the 20th century.

To many observers at the time, it appeared that the family and morality had broken down. Another cultural crisis ensued, until a new cultural blueprint emerged—the companionate model of marriage and the family. The new model reconciled older Victorian ideals with a more informal and sexualized version of the marriage bond.

This highly abbreviated history of family and cultural change forms the necessary backdrop for understanding the family upheavals of the late 20th century. As in early times, a set of major changes in economy and society destabilized an existing paradigm of family life, and the everyday patterns and practices that sustained them. . . .

## Wives Become Companions and Equals

In historical perspective, the breadwinner-housewife type of family most people in the West define as *traditional* is actually an uncommon arrangement. It is associated with the early stages of the industrial revolution, when, as noted earlier, work first moved out of the home and the family ceased to be an economic unit. . . . The breadwinner family develops slowly in the early stages of industrialization, characterizing the growing but still small middle class. Then, after reaching a peak in which very few married women are employed, it declines. More and more women find work in a growing service sector—in offices, schools, hospitals, stores. . . .

| | | | | | | | | Average population |
|---|---|---|---|---|---|---|---|---|
| Year | 1 person | 2 persons | 3 persons | 4 persons | 5 persons | 6 persons | 7 or more persons | per household |
| 1790 (Mar.) | 3.7% | 7.8% | 11.7% | 13.8% | 13.9% | 13.2% | 35.8% | — |
| 1890 (June) | 3.6 | 13.2 | 16.7 | 16.8 | 15.1 | 11.6 | 23.0 | 4.93 |
| 1900 (Mar.) | 5.1 | 15.0 | 17.6 | 16.9 | 14.2 | 10.9 | 20.4 | — |
| 1930 (Apr.) | 7.9 | 23.4 | 20.8 | 17.5 | 12.0 | 7.6 | 10.9 | 4.11 |
| 1940 (Apr.) | 7.1 | 24.8 | 22.4 | 18.1 | 11.5 | 6.8 | 9.3 | 3.67 |
| 1950 (Apr.)[1] | 10.9 | 28.8 | 22.6 | 17.8 | 10.0 | 5.1 | 4.9 | 3.37 |
| 1960 (Mar.) | 13.1 | 27.8 | 18.9 | 17.6 | 11.5 | 5.7 | 5.4 | 3.35 |
| 1970 (Mar.) | 17.0 | 28.8 | 17.3 | 15.8 | 10.4 | 5.6 | 5.1 | 3.14 |
| 1980 (Mar.) | 22.7 | 31.3 | 17.5 | 15.7 | 7.5 | 3.1 | 2.2 | 2.76 |
| 1990 (Mar.) | 24.6 | 32.2 | 17.2 | 15.5 | 6.7 | 2.3 | 1.4 | 2.63 |
| 2000 (Mar.) | 25.5 | 33.1 | 16.4 | 14.6 | 6.7 | 2.3 | 1.4 | 2.62 |
| 2004 (Mar.)[2] | 26.4 | 33.4 | 16.0 | 14.3 | 6.4 | 2.2 | 1.2 | 2.57 |

**Households by size, 1790–2004**

*Percent distribution of number of households*

1. Covers related persons only; therefore, not strictly comparable with other years.
2. Based on Census 2000 and an expanded sample of households.

TAKEN FROM: "Households by size, 1790–2004." Data taken from the U.S. Census Bureau: www.census.gov.

The transformation of a housewife into a paid worker outside the home sends tremors through every family relationship. It creates a more symmetrical family, undoing the sharp dichotomy between roles that characterizes the breadwinner-housewife pattern. It also increases the opportunity costs of pregnancy and childrearing and reduces women's economic dependence on men, thereby making it easier for women to leave unhappy marriages. . . .

## Death Disrupts Families

The widespread myth of a golden past of family stability is in large part a product of public unawareness of the feature of family life, and daily life in general, in the past that most sets it off from our own era—the omnipresence and visibility of death.

In earlier times, most mortality took place in infancy, but death remained an ever-present possibility at any age. It was not unusual for young and middle aged adults to die of tuberculous, pneumonia, or other infectious diseases. Before the turn of [the 20th] century, only 40% of women lived through all the stages of a "normal" life course—growing up, marrying, having children, and surviving with a spouse to the age of 50.

Today, by contrast, despite accidents, disease, crime, environmental pollution, and stress, most people in modern societies go about their business on the assumption they will live out a full life. Today, death at any time before old age has become a rare event; about 75% of all deaths occur after the age of 65.

These simple changes in mortality rates had a profound effect on family life. [Sociology professor] Peter Uhlenberg examined the impact of mortality change on various aspects of family life by contrasting mortality rates in 1900 with those of 1976. He found that under 1900 conditions, half of all parents experienced the death of a child. By 1976, only 6% did. In the conditions of the early 20th century, more than half of all children who lived to the age of 15 experienced a death in the immediate family—either a parent or a sibling.

When death could strike adults at any age, large numbers of children experienced orphanhood. In 1900, about 1 out of 14 children lost a parent before the age of 15, 1 out of 62 lost both. In 1976, only 1 out of 20 lost one parent by age 15, 1 out of 1,800 lost both. Because so many children were orphaned in the early 20th century, the chances that a child was not living with either parent was greater than it is now. Indeed, some of the current growth in single-parent families is offset by a decline in the number of children raised in institutions, foster homes, or by relatives. . . .

## The (Frequent) Survival of (Fewer) Children

Another effect of shifting mortality rates is that the death of a child is no longer a sad but normal hazard of parenthood. Rather, it has become a devastating, life-shattering loss from which the parents may never fully recover. The intense emotional bonding between parents and infants we take for granted today, and see as a sociobiological given, became the norm only in the 18th and 19th centuries. The privileged classes created the modern "emotionally priceless" child, a powerful ideal which gradually filtered down through the rest of society.

Another major result of falling death rates is a decline in fertility rates. By granting parents confidence that they did not have to have "extra" children to ensure that some would survive to adulthood, lowered mortality rates in early childhood encouraged careful planning of births and smaller families. The combination of longer lives and fewer, closely spaced children created a still-lengthening "empty nest" stage of the family. This in turn encouraged the companionate style of marriage, which focuses on the relationship between husband and wife; this shift in the meaning and function of marriages may have a good deal to do with the increase in divorce.

## Family Today: Changed but Cherished

In sum, reductions in mortality have encouraged stronger emotional bonds between parents and children, lengthened the duration of marriage and parent-child relationships, made grandparenthood an expectable stage of the life course, and increased the number of grandparents children actually know. . . .

At the same time, lengthened life spans have increased the number of frail elderly and made chronic rather than infectious disease the leading causes of death. Contrary to the myth of the "abandoned" elderly, adult children (mostly daughters) remain the primary caregivers to the elderly. The big change is that people in the past were far less likely to be called upon to care for an aging parent, because few people lived to be old and frail. . . .

The multiple social transformations of this era have brought both costs and benefits: Family relations became more fragile and more emotionally rich; mass longevity has brought us a host of problems as well as the gift of extended life. Change brought greater opportunities for women, but because of persisting gender inequality, women bore a large share of the costs. But we cannot turn the clock back to the family models of the past. Furthermore, despite nostalgia for the world we have lost, few of us would actually want to return to conditions of life endured by most people in generations past.

Paradoxically, after all the upheavals of the recent decades, the emotional and cultural significance of the family persists. Family remains the center of most people's lives, and as numerous surveys show, a cherished value.

*"The face of the family has not changed
so much as it seems."*

# Traditional Families Are Fundamentally Unchanged

*Jennie Bristow*

*Jennie Bristow, a journalist in the United Kingdom, writes extensively about family, politics, culture, and other issues facing the modern era. In this viewpoint, she explores the seeming contradictions in the current state of the family. The author proposes the idea that, although the family structure seems to be very different than in previous decades, it is still performing the same social and personal functions that it always has. What has changed is how society views its responsibility to the family and how people consider family to be important to their well-being.*

As you read, consider the following questions:

1. Historically, what benefits did the family provide to individuals and to society?

2. What two groups of people are supposedly engaged in the "mommy wars"?

3. What social philosophy has enabled the traditional family to survive cultural upheaval?

Jennie Bristow, "What Future for the Family?: Behind the 'Mommy Wars' and the New Politics of the Family," *www.spiked-online.com*, November 17, 2004. Copyright © 2000–2006. All rights reserved. Reproduced by permission.

Families, it is generally agreed, are more complicated than they have ever been before. Long gone are the days of breadwinner dad, housewife mum, and the obligatory 2.4 children. The falling marriage rate and the high divorce rate, the declining fertility rate and the rising number of working mothers, the cultural tolerance of homosexuality, atheism, singledom, abortion, childlessness, artificial insemination, lone parenthood and what used to be called 'living in sin' all reflect a society in which, on the face of it, it no longer seems possible to take 'the family' for granted.

But have things really changed so dramatically? Despite the changing face of the family, it is still the way in which most people live. The family remains an institution that plays a key role in the way society is organised and controlled, and which adapts, not to the whims of individuals, but to the conflicting priorities placed upon it by the world at large. In fact, the major shift in modern Western society has been not in the family itself, but in the culture surrounding it. While it is accepted that the family does, and should, play a central role in nurturing individuals and raising children, there is a growing ambivalence about people's capacity to succeed at this task.

In policy circles, 'diversity', 'understanding' and 'supporting' are the buzzwords for discussions about the family, as though it is no longer possible to expect that, left to their own devices, families will be able to sustain themselves. In corporate and media circles, concerns about 'juggling' the conflicting priorities of the 'work-life balance' lead to versatile dilemma commentary on the business and parenting pages. In the book world, the 'mommy wars' pitches stay-home moms defensively fighting the domestic corner against guilt-tripped career mothers who want to feel better about their ambitions and their kids and less bad about themselves. . . .

## Family Is the Foundation of Society

'You know, there is no such thing as society', proclaimed former UK prime minister Margaret Thatcher in 1987. 'There are individual men and women, and there are families.' This notorious matter-of-fact quote contained a wealth of meaning, about the centrality of the family to the operation of capitalism and the problem of the family as a bulwark against social change.

So far as Thatcher was concerned, the world turned upon the work of individuals, and the role played by their families in both sustaining these individuals and dampening their desire for risk-taking and rebellion. . . .

Ever since Frederick Engels famously exposed 'The origin of the family, private property and the state' in the late nineteenth century, it has been possible to understand the nuclear family as something that is not natural, God-given or chosen, but a product of particular historical circumstances. Engels' seminal text traced the conditions that gave rise to different forms of family life and state structure in different societies. He discussed, for example, how different types of marriage 'corresponded broadly to the three principal stages of human development: for the period of savagery, group marriage; for barbarism, pairing marriage; for civilisation, monogamy'.

Civilisation is 'the stage of development in society at which the division of labour, the exchange between individuals arising from it, and the commodity production which combines them both come to their full growth and revolutionise the whole of previous society'. It marks a major shift in the relationship between man and nature, allowing humanity to transcend the limitations imposed by the biological division of labour common to previous societies. The form taken by the family, at this juncture, is not simply a continuation of past living arrangements according to natural laws, but a social and economic institution that plays a key role in the maintenance and reproduction of civilised, capitalist society.

The family is the basis for the reproduction of the working class. It provides a space in which the wage-earner can be nourished and cared for, given some respite from the physical demands and the emotional void of the workplace, and in which he will have and raise children. The creation of a private sphere of life, outside of the direct rule of the state and the market, gives the wage-earner a necessary sense of autonomy and control, along with a myriad of private responsibilities and emotional concerns that bolster his commitment to work and his desire for stability. . . .

## Has the Family Really Changed?

Watch daytime TV. Visit a provincial shopping centre on a Saturday. Buy a house, a car, a holiday, and there is no doubt that the nuclear family still exists. In private households all over the UK, parents are raising their children, cooking the dinner, doing the washing and working to pay the bills.

On paper, the family today certainly looks different, even as compared with 30 years ago. The latest edition of *Social Trends*, produced by the UK Office for National Statistics, presents some startling figures. In the UK in 2002, almost 41 per cent of all children were born outside marriage. The proportion of UK households comprising a couple with dependent children fell from around a third in 1971 to just over one-fifth in spring 2003. Over the same period, the proportion of lone-parent households with dependent children almost doubled, now accounting for five per cent of households. The marriage rate continues to fall and there are about the same number of divorces as there are first marriages. Increasing numbers of women are choosing not to reproduce at all. Eleven per cent of women born in 1925 were still childless at age 35; this more than doubled to 25 per cent for women aged 35 born in 1965, and it is expected that this trend will continue.

But while these are important changes, none of them suggests that the family itself has transformed, merely that more people are opting out of family life. And when the figures are looked at another way, it is possible to argue that even the face of the family has not changed so much as it seems. Two-

# Is the Family in Decline?

The recent [as of 2003] trends of various demographic indicators of family life may, at first sight, seem to confirm that the traditional family is about to vanish: nuptiality and fertility are decreasing, while consensual unions, LAT-relations [Living Apart Together], union disruptions, single person households are increasing.

While it may be argued that the strong decline in nuptiality rates is indicative of a loss of appeal of a certain type of legally regulated partnership, they do not necessarily foreshadow the disappearance of the family. . . . Evidence from a variety of sources shows that most people establish an enduring relationship and eventually marry. Moreover, investigations have shown that cohabiting couples strongly resemble married couples in many ways.

An increase in divorces may be interpreted as a threat to the continued existence of the family. It may be argued that present levels of divorce rather reflect the difference in gender expectations with respect to partnership than a rejection of enduring relationships. Research shows that most divorced people want to, and do, establish new, enduring relationships. . . .

A nuanced analysis of demographic data reveals the shallowness of 'the death of the family' scenario based on a quick reading of statistics. But even stronger arguments against the disappearance scenario are found in human biology. After all, human beings have been selected—for reproductive ends—to form enduring, not necessarily lifelong, sexual bonds. Indeed, there is ample evidence that in modern culture, where a wider range of relational options has become available, the vast majority of the population continues to want to develop enduring relationships.

*Robert Cliquet, "The Disappearance of the Family,"*
Major Trends Affecting Family in the New Millennium—
Western Europe and North America. *Report for United Nations
Department of Economic and Social Affairs, 2003.*

fifths of children are born outside marriage—but in 2002, nearly 64 per cent of all births outside marriage were jointly registered by parents living at the same address, more than twice the proportion in 1986. This suggests that these are stable monogamous relationships, if not married ones. While both the age of first childbirth and the proportion of women remaining childless are rising, the average number of children women think they will have is still around two per woman. The marriage rate is falling but there has been an increase in cohabitation: among non-married women aged under 60, the proportion cohabiting more than doubled from 13 per cent in 1986 to 28 per cent in 2001/02. For men it also more than doubled over the same period, from 12 per cent to 25 per cent.

## Working Mothers and the Family

One major change to the traditional family has of course been the increase in women working. The idea of the male bread-winner and the family wage seems outmoded, and it is now assumed that women will be something other than house-wives. It is now normal to be a working mother, and improve-ments in daycare and employment policy have made working and raising children a real possibility. But daycare is still ex-pensive, inflexible and patchily provided, and the statistics in-dicate that working motherhood is less common than it might be assumed. Among married or cohabiting women with a child under five, only 19 per cent work full time; rising to 41 per cent—well under half—by the time the youngest child is 16. For lone mothers, the figures are 10 per cent and 46 per cent respectively.

Far from 'having it all'—the career, the husband, the kids—it seems that working motherhood, for many women, means a part-time job, pin money and some activity outside the home. This is less about full engagement in the public sphere than about the kind of job 'on the side' that working-class women have for decades been forced to take to boost the family income.

A detailed analysis of this data would raise interesting insights and questions. But even this brief overview indicates that there has been no major transformation of the family that approaches the shift that Engels identified from barbarism to civilisation. What has changed is not the composition of the family, or the way in which families operate. They still raise their kids and do the housework in private, and in most cases it is still the woman who does the lion's share of the domestic work. The key shift has been in the politics of the family. . . .

## The New Politics of the Family

In *The Mommy Myth: The Idealisation of Motherhood and How It Has Undermined Women*, US academics Susan J. Douglas and Meredith W. Michaels hark back fondly to a world where housewives demanded wages, working mothers demanded daycare centres with dry-cleaners attached, and everybody recognised that women had A Bad Lot. They wonder whatever happened to feminism, to socialism, to the notion that there must be other ways of treating women and raising children than the paltry choice between full-on privatised motherhood and the guilty work-family juggling on offer in society today. . . .

*The Mommy Myth* is one of the recent books to come out of the 'mommy wars' currently being fought on both sides of the Atlantic. In the USA, this takes the form of a pitched battle between smug middle-class stay-home moms, loyally sacrificing themselves on the altar of child-rearing and fretting about their loss of personal identity and social capital, and ambitious middle-class career moms holding down a demanding job and a full burden of guilt. In the UK, it takes the more muted form of journalists writing confessional books about how strange and difficult motherhood really is, and pragmatic, convoluted debates about the problem of finding the right 'work-life balance'. Insofar as there is any discussion outside of policy circles about the politics of the family, the mommy wars is it; and it represents just how confused this debate has become.

The mommy wars are phoney. It is not that career moms really blame stay-home moms for their guilt, or vice versa. Rather, these arguments highlight the cultural ambivalence that currently surrounds family life. Nobody now thinks . . . that family life is all there is. From cradle to college, women are taught about the importance of preserving individual identity and the pitfalls of staying home with the kids. But nor is there any sense, any more, that women can 'have it all'—the career, the kids, the lifestyle. When it comes to the tension between the public world of work and the private world of the family, the word of the decade is 'juggling'. . . .

## Parents Commit to Children and the Family Endures

The dilemma of the 'mommy wars' is summed up by US academic Sharon Hays in her powerful 1996 book *The Cultural Contradictions of Motherhood*. Through in-depth interviews with stay-home and working mothers across social classes, Hays argues that the desirability, and actuality, of women's increased participation in the labour market has been complemented by the aggressive promotion of a philosophy of 'intensive mothering', which preaches the need for the parent—whatever their working situation—to hold the real and supposed needs of the child paramount.

The success of this philosophy is what has allowed the family to survive, even in the face of the pressures placed upon it by women leaving the home and playing a significant role in the public world. By continually emphasising the need to put the child first—even if this involves paying for the best-quality daycare and packing in the quality time at home—parents' (and particularly, mothers') commitment to their private responsibilities is ensured.

*"The ability to love and commit to another person is a right that all people have."*

# Same-Sex Marriage Should Be Allowed

## Heather Ann Gannon

*Heather Ann Gannon originally wrote this viewpoint for a political science class at the University of Hawaii, but went on to publish it in* Hohonu: A Journal of Academic Writing. *In it, Gannon explains the logic behind three popular arguments against legalizing same-sex marriage and then argues against them. Ultimately, the author makes the case that the American ideals of equal protection and equal opportunity demand that same-sex couples have the right to marry that opposite-sex couples enjoy.*

As you read, consider the following questions:

1. What is the primary flaw in the religious argument against same-sex marriage?
2. What is the significance of procreation to the modern institution of marriage?

3. How has the definition of marriage evolved throughout history?

It is difficult to articulate why I think that same-sex couples should have the right to marry. To say that they should have this right because they are just as deserving as opposite-sex couples seems to be a cheap and flimsy argument, because it implies the possibility that same-sex couples may not meet some arbitrary standard. The Supreme Court has declared that marriage is a basic civil right, older than the Constitution itself. When civil rights are at stake there is no such thing as deserving them; they are intrinsic to our very way of life. Marriage seems as basic to me as the freedom of religion or of speech. Most people don't question why we have freedom of religion or speech; we have these rights because all free people have them, because it is wrong for the government to infringe upon them. This is what our country was founded on. Therefore, I choose to look at reasons why it is argued that same-sex couples should NOT have the right to marry and then to show those contentions to be shallow and weak arguments when held against the principles that we, as Americans, hold dear.

## Debunking the Religious Argument

The first argument that is used in attempting to curtail the rights of same-sex couples is a religious one. Those who take this tack argue that the Bible says that homosexuality is a sin. Because homosexuality is a sin, we should not encourage homosexual relationships by recognizing their unions. At first glance, this argument seems relatively logical. The Bible does say that homosexuality is a sin. No less than nine Bible verses attest to the sinfulness of homosexuality. The Bible even goes so far as to label homosexuality an abomination, which, as a noted biblical scholar notes, is the worst category of sin, reserved for only those practices that are most abhorrent to

# A Conservative Christian Supports Civil Same-Sex Marriage

Christians need to take a second look at [the issue of gay marriage]. . . . Homosexuals are the only group of people in American society who are legally barred from marriage. As long as the state refuses to recognize same-sex marriage, they cannot legally marry the person they love. . . .

If you are a homosexual adult . . . the only kind of marriage that can be legitimately granted to you is one you must enter into dishonestly, swearing before God and these witnesses to a love you don't really have.

But the kind of marriage homosexuals seek doesn't even involve swearing before God and these witnesses. What they want is a secular marriage granted and recognized by the state, and we can keep the religious institution of marriage homosexual-free. . . .

People think that by allowing civil same-sex marriage, it won't be long before we'll allow people to marry their sister, or their pet iguana. But isn't there a big difference between a person who chooses incest or bestiality against the normal marriage options available to him, and a person who is only capable of being sexually attracted to someone of the same gender, so that without the right to enter into same-sex marriage he or she is left with no marriage option at all? People who like having sex with family members or dumb animals are making perverse sexual choices. By contrast the vast majority of homosexuals did not choose to be homosexual.

*Misty S. Irons, "A Conservative Christian Case for Civil Same-Sex Marriage," 2004. www.musingson.com.*

God. Surely, then, for God-fearing Christians, it is their duty to stop the promulgation of this abominable act as much as possible.

There are two immediate problems with this argument. The first speaks to the religious aspect of the view. While homosexuality is a sin, according to the Bible, there are other sins that are just as bad. Specifically, idol worship and murder are considered abominations along with homosexuality. Neither of these other definitions of abomination are used to restrict access to marriage. Indeed, the Supreme Court has allowed convicted felons to marry. Idolaters are also not restricted in their ability to marry.

This leads directly into the second problem with this argument. Marriage in the United States is a civil affair. There is no state that requires a religious service to be married. Judges and authorized civil servants can perform a marriage ceremony in every state. In Colorado the couple themselves can obtain a marriage license and solemnize the marriage themselves, by signing the license and returning it back to the County Clerk. Some states allow family or friends to solemnize the marriage. No deity needs to be invoked for marriage to happen; there are no specific words that must be spoken. All that need happen is that the couple say that they intend to take each other as spouses. As much as some people might like the laws to reflect their moral or religious views, the laws are for everyone, even those that do not share their views.

## Debunking the Procreation Argument

Another common argument for the current ban on same-sex marriage is that marriage is for procreation. Marriage is the foundation of our society, insofar as it involves the getting and rearing of the next generation. Furthermore, the argument continues, a two parent, opposite sex household is the most stable and therefore preferable environment for raising happy, healthy children. Same sex-couples are biologically incapable of conceiving children; therefore, they are rationally exempt from the institution that protects this vital building block of society.

This argument sounds logical at first. Marriage, however, is no longer (if it ever was) primarily for the conception and raising of children. It is all about the closeness and companionship of two people. Many married couples decide not to have children, even though they are biologically capable of producing them. The Supreme Court has repeatedly ruled that couples have the right to decide when and if to have children. Fertility tests are not required before getting a marriage license in any state. The right to marry has been upheld even in cases where conceiving a child would be impossible, including when the woman is beyond child-bearing age, when a partner is on their death bed, and convicted convicts still in jail. Some states, including Illinois and Utah, allow first cousins to marry only if they can prove that one or both of the parties is unable to produce children.

The second half of this argument, that two parent households with one parent of each sex is the best way to rear children, is also specious. Today many states allow same-sex couples to adopt children. Furthermore, growing up in a traditional mother and father two parent home doesn't guarantee a happy, or even a safe, childhood. As many as one-third of abused children come from two parent homes. Even those who have proven they cannot take care of their children are not banned from marrying. In *Zablocki v. Redhall*, the Supreme Court ruled that deadbeat fathers could not be banned from marriage. One's fitness to raise children is not and never has been a consideration in getting a marriage license. Given this, the argument that marriage is to ensure the next generation fails to convince.

## Debunking the Historical Argument

The third consideration I will look at is history. Throughout our recorded history, marriage has taken place mostly between one man and one woman. A goodly number of people take this to mean that marriage between a man and a woman is natural, whereas union between two people of the same sex is unnatural. The common law definition of marriage, as articulated by the Massachusetts Supreme Court in 1974 as well as the Federal Defense of Marriage Act in 1996, is a union between one man and one woman. Because marriage has been traditionally defined for opposite sex couples, same sex couples are automatically excluded from it. Marriage may be a civil right, but marriage between people of the same sex is not. This is the argument that the New Jersey Supreme Court used when upholding the ban on same sex marriages in that state earlier this month [in 2003].

All of these things may be true. However, once upon a time, not so very long ago, marriage was considered a contract between two men. Women went from being the non-entity of child to being the non-entity of wife. Women had no right to property or even to her children, because she existed only as an adjunct to her husband. Women were treated as property, and their consent was not required for a marriage to be legal. In addition, just in this last century, marriage was defined as a union between people of the same race. In 1967, for example, sixteen states had anti-miscegenation laws on the books, making marriage between two people of different races a criminal offense. At that time it was considered unnatural for the races to marry, much the same way society views same-sex marriages today. The argument that history is a valid consideration may not be valid in any case. . . . The Supreme Court struck down the ban on sodomy laws in this nation. In the majority opinion, the Court said that tradition was not a not valid reason for discriminatory laws. History shows us that everything, including our definition of marriage, changes over time.

The ability to love and commit to another person is a right that all people have. It is not something that can be granted to us, and cannot be taken away. The state can choose to recognize those commitments, or it can choose not to. Our country's history is one of increasing the rights and liberties that we, as a people, have. It is one of inclusion, not exclusion. The Massachusetts Supreme Court apparently agrees with me. On November 18th [2003] they issued a long awaited ruling in the case of *Goodridge v. Dept. of Public Health.* The long and short of the opinion is that the ban on gay marriages in the state of Massachusetts [would end] in 6 months, unless the legislature [did] something to prevent it. In the majority opinion, the court used many of the arguments I have presented here to define and justify its decision. It is wrong to disallow a segment of our society access to one of our society's defining institutions because of one characteristic that they have. It goes against our ideals of equal protection and equal opportunity for all under the laws.

| *"Marriage is more than a loving relationship between two people."*

# Same-Sex Marriage Should Not Be Allowed

## Donald DeMarco

*Dr. Donald DeMarco is a professor of philosophy at Holy Apostles College and Seminary in Connecticut and a prolific author of books and articles addressing Catholicism, reproduction, the value of human life, and moral virtue. In the following viewpoint, DeMarco makes a case against legalizing same-sex marriage. He argues that heterosexual marriage and the children that result from such a union contribute to the stability of Western civilization. The author further argues that homosexual love is naturally inferior to heterosexual love.*

As you read, consider the following questions:

1. When did the perception of homosexuality change from acceptable to abominable?

2. According to the author, what is biologically special about heterosexual intercourse?

3. On what grounds does the article conclude that same-sex marriage should be disallowed?

Donald DeMarco, "Same-Sex Marriage," *The Family in America: Online Edition*, Swan Library of Family Culture, April, 2001. Copyright © 1997–2006 The Howard Center. Reproduced by permission.

The Metropolitan Community Church of Toronto (MCC) is part of the Universal Fellowship of Metropolitan Community Churches, headquartered in West Hollywood, California. The MCC has let it be known that it will be performing "legal" same-sex marriages on a regular basis, effective January 2001.

In response to MCC plans, Consumer Minister Bob Runciman has stated that Ontario will not recognize such marriages. He cites Canadian federal law which requires that a *legal* marriage must be the union of a man and a woman.

An editorial in the *Toronto Star* (Dec. 7, 2000) argues that the MCC plan is "groundbreaking" and compares it with the suffragette movement, as many view the matter as simply one of *equality of rights*. Some have characterized any opposition to same-sex marriages as "homophobic" and "right wing."

## Heterosexuality Drives Western Civilization

Looking at the issue from an historical perspective, we see that homosexual acts were largely accepted in ancient times. It was the Jewish *Torah* that found it to be an "abomination." It was Judaism alone, 3,000 years ago, which denounced homosexual practices, while insisting that all sexual activity be channeled into marriage, a two-in-one flesh union between a man and a woman. In other words, it was marriage as a faithful and intimate union between a man and a woman that was truly groundbreaking. Moreover, this form of marriage, together with its resulting family, has been a source of great strength and stability for Western civilization. Jewish scholar Dennis Prager has remarked that. . . .

> The acceptance of homosexuality as the equal of heterosexual love signifies the decline of Western civilization as surely as the rejection of homosexuality and other non-marital sex made the creation of this civilization possible.

## Gay Marriage vs. American Marriage

Human beings have come up with almost as many ways of getting hitched as they have languages to tell mother-in-law jokes. . . .

But beneath all the diversity, marriage has always had a fundamental, universal core that makes gay marriage a non sequitur: it has always governed property and inheritance rights; it has always been the means of establishing paternity, legitimacy, and the rights and responsibilities of parenthood; and because these goals involve bearing and raising children, it has always involved (at least one) man and woman. What's more, among the "startling diversity" of variations that different cultures have elaborated on this fundamental core, our own culture has produced a specifically American ideal of marriage that is inseparable from our vision of free citizenship and is deeply embedded in our history, politics, economics, and culture.

*Kay S. Hymowitz.*
*"Gay Marriage vs. American Marriage,"*
*City Journal, Summer 2004.*

Marriage is more than a loving relationship between two people. Love is not restricted by gender, age, race, social status, etc. Love is universal. However, marriage is subject to restrictions, precisely because of its nature as a two-in-one flesh union. Whereas each person is equally lovable by another, it cannot be said that each person is equally marriageable for that other. The essence of marriage is not equality, but two human beings who are properly proportioned to each other in accordance with the nature of marriage. As an institution, marriage transcends individuality or personal will or political fiat.

## Marriage Is Defined by Biology

The science of immunology provides important insights that help us to understand why a same-sex relationship cannot exemplify a two-in-one flesh intimacy. An individual's immune system contains 100 billion immunological receptors. Each of these receptors has the remarkable capacity to distinguish the *self* from the *non-self*. In this way, the immune system protects the self from the intrusion of anything that is foreign and potentially dangerous to it. The immune system not only fights off diseases, but is also set up to reject organ transplants, since it recognizes the transplanted organ as something alien to it. From a purely immunological standpoint, we are all alien to each other.

During heterosexual intercourse, something very special takes place immunologically. The male semen contains a mild immunosuppressant which, when released into the woman's body, alters her immune system just enough so that the man's sperm is received as part of herself. This acceptance and mutual identification on an immunological level is also necessary to prevent the woman's body from rejecting an ensuing embryo as if it were a foreign substance. In other words, through sexual union, a man and a woman truly achieve a two-in-one flesh unity. The child that is formed as a result of their union is the fruit of that union. An intimate union of this kind is not possible between same-sex couples.

## True Marriage Leads to Parenthood

The nature of heterosexual intercourse is uniquely ordered so that the male and female participants are not only profoundly united to each other—body and soul—but involve themselves in an act through which they can confer upon each other the blessing of motherhood and fatherhood. This is why marriage, in the truest sense, requires a man and a woman. People who are of the same sex can love each other, be friends, or remain lifelong allies. They cannot, however, be married to each other according to a two-in-one flesh intimacy that is intrinsically ordered to parenthood.

This is not a political restriction, but one that is natural. We cannot de-legislate nature by a political act.

*"Today's widespread tendency to assume that the needs of small children can only be taken care of by their biological mothers is of fairly recent origin."*

# Working Mothers Have Enough Time to Raise Children

**Brigitte Berger**

*Brigitte Berger is a professor emerita of sociology at Boston University. The following viewpoint, which first appeared in the book* The Family in the Modern Age, *explains how women struggle to balance their personal interests with the welfare of their families. The author writes that even working women find themselves heavily investing their time and energy in their homes and children and that throughout history women—working and otherwise—have always had assistance with childcare and childrearing.*

As you read, consider the following questions:

1. What are some reasons that women enter the workforce?

Brigitte Berger, "Critical Contemporary Issues," *The Family in the Modern Age: More than a Lifestyle Choice.* Piscataway, NJ: Transaction Publishers, 2002, pp. 195–98. Copyright © 2002 by Transaction Publishers. Reprinted by permission of Transaction Publishers and Copyright Clearance.

2. What factors first encouraged middle-class families to become directly involved with childrearing and socialization?

3. How do working mothers find more time to spend with their children?

The reasons why women enter the paid labor force are many. They range from the wish to make money to a quest for autonomy and self-fulfillment, from escape from boredom to genuine career interests, from desires for individual achievement to those for making a contribution to knowledge and society at large. Some, though surprisingly few, opt for having only a career or only staying home. The majority hopes that they can "have it all": a family as well as a career.

The contradictory nature of their values places women into a peculiar quandary: since they are committed to participate and stay in the labor force—and there is little indication that this will change significantly anytime soon—few are ready to quit the workplace on a permanent basis when family needs arise. Most oscillate between periods in which desires for personal autonomy and having a career are replaced by even more powerful desires for having a family and a home. What is more, this observed shift in priorities might be repeated more than once during the lifetime of a given individual. Indeed, women go to enormous lengths to prepare themselves for a career only to discover that in most cases love for children and for family comes to take precedence. Yet once they think they have the most pressing needs of their children under control, the lure of the workplace gains in strength once more. Juggling between two worlds, that of the family and that of work, they frequently make heroic efforts to do justice to both. While desperately clinging to their autonomy, they also try to contribute to the emotional and economic well-being of their families. Some take up jobs that permit easy exit from and reentry into the labor market or that offer op-

## No One Does It All

"How do you do it all?"

I often get this question, and my answer is this: no one does it all. *Doing it all* means, of course, having a career and having kids, and it's one of the great myths of our era. The myth is that you can pursue these two essentially incompatible activities without screwing up either one. The myth is that having children will infuse your professional work with a wondrous energy (akin to the fabled second-trimester glow) *and* that having a job will make you a more interesting and fulfilled person, and thus a better parent.

A strange conversational dance occurs when two women meet and begin finding out who works and who stays at home. . . . Why does it matter? There's a "mommy war" going on, and members of each side often feel more comfortable with other women who have made choices like theirs. Furthermore, we are often eager to validate our own decisions as the best ones for our children.

*Ellen Lupton, "The Myth of the Working Mom,"*
*AIGA: Writing Web Site, September 12, 2006.*
*www.aiga.org/content.cfm/the-myth-of-the-working-mom.*

portunities for part-time and flexible work schedules and that, in sum, can be reconciled to a lifeplan in which the family plays a central role. Others embark on a life of doing double-shift duty. In some rough-botched union between work and family most women, in their own ways, seek to make the best of a very difficult situation. They love their husbands, children, and their larger family by extension, but will sometimes sacrifice them all a bit (along with themselves) for the sake of work and vice versa. The new lifestyle of turn-of-the-twentieth-century [in the early 2000s] mothers involves more often than not the necessity to secure some forms of paid childcare, though they worry a great deal whether they are doing right by their children.

## Childrearing in History

The fact that women of all social classes are today much less likely to slow down for their pregnancies and much more likely to continue to stay in the paid labor force has provided cultural pundits of all stripes with yet further evidence of an uncaring individualism on the rise. This is an accusation that reveals a good deal of historical ignorance. Today's widespread tendency to assume that the needs of small children can only be taken care of by their biological mothers is of fairly recent origin. To be sure, households in the past were larger than today, with all sorts of people milling about who could be expected to keep an eye on children and for the more well-to-do the help of servants was always available. Yet as the French social historian Jacques Donzelot has been able to document, two major considerations—the one relating to the mind and the other to the body—encouraged the rising middle classes of the nineteenth century to become directly involved in the rearing and socialization of their offspring. Leaving the care of children to servants and other hired help, as it had been the custom of the well-to-do for long, was increasingly rejected as it was held to have a deleterious influence on a child's acquisition of desirable character traits. At the same time, an emerging core of medical professionals spread the message that the hygienic and nutritional requirements of children could best be met within a parentally controlled environment. This growing conviction about what it takes to prepare children to acquire the habits and the knowledge to compete in an increasingly achievement-oriented social order turned childrearing into the rising bourgeoisie's primary task and mission. It was precisely this preoccupation with the child's well-being and development that set the socialization patterns of the growing middle classes apart from those of the aristocracy as well as the lower social ranks. With their reliance upon servants, wet nurses, tutors, and the like, the first continued the soon-to-be discredited routines of the past, while the latter neither had the leisure nor the knowledge to reflect upon the inadequacies of the childrearing practices of a rapidly disappearing rural world. And for those who had migrated to the cities in search of work and opportunities, it would take some time to adapt themselves fully to the new patterns of modern social life.

At the same time, it is of some importance to keep in mind that although a child's well-being and progress was central in the life of the middle-class family, at no time did the nurture and socialization of children exclusively depend upon the biological mother. Those who could afford it made use of the services of hired help in easing the pressures created by the routine tasks of middle-class housekeeping, and when it came to their children's schooling, it was taken for granted that only the most competent and inspired teachers would do. The all-encompassing mission of childrearing and housekeeping, incidentally, provided middle-class women with new forms of power and status. In the vast literature on the evolving childrearing practices in the modern order, Frank Musgrove's *Youth and the Social Order* stands out for the clarity of the description of the social class dimensions in this area of social life.

## Working Mothers Make Time for Children

Though it has become fashionable of late to pronounce that it "takes a village" to raise a child, the combined insights of two hundred years show that it takes a great deal more to bring up a child in the contemporary industrial world than a reliance on the simple networks of an imagined rural past. Modern childrearing is an exceedingly strenuous, time-consuming, and intellectually demanding task. It demands the establishment of a congenial yet organized family environment in which children are allowed to develop their very individual talents and competencies and to acquire those virtues that make for decency and responsibility. By definition almost, it must be very individualistically oriented, and it requires the love and devotion only a father and a mother are able to provide.

That said, it is also of great importance to recognize that the shift in contemporary work patterns that takes both fathers and mothers out of the home does not imply that today's parents do not meet their parental duties. Though it was admittedly easier in the past to provide for a stable home and close supervision when mothers stayed at home, the new practices do not invariably spell doom for the future of their children. Perhaps even more than their predecessors, present-day mothers and fathers are striving with all the strength and means at their disposal to ensure their children's well-being, happiness, and progress. So, for instance, the amount of time mothers report spending with their children in 1998 has not changed over the past forty years despite the fact that three-fourths of the women with children younger than eighteen are in the workforce today [as of 2002]. In reply to the question of how working mothers find the time, the author of the study, the sociologist Suzanne Bianchi, reports that today's working mothers sleep five or six hours less each week than mothers who are not employed, and they have up to twelve fewer hours of free time at their personal disposal. They also vacuum less. In other words, today's conventional parents are in no way different from their predecessors, if anything, they work harder and worry more. To be sure, to provide for their children's physical and supervisory needs, many may have to rely to a greater degree upon out-of-the home care by strangers over whom they may have little control. Yet to a far greater degree than in the past, today's parents are fully cognizant of the importance of providing children with sound fundamentals, the capacity for individual judgment, and with skills and values that prepare them for an unknown future. Some current parental practices and arrangements may appear to be misguided to some present-day observers. Yet as long as they meet basic requirements for safety and individualized care and an abundance of love, the current problematization of every childrearing issue flowing from a mother's decision to stay in the labor force and have a career appears to be superfluous.

*"Parents cannot invest the same amount of time in learning all the detailed particular things about the individual child if they are spending the majority of their waking hours away from the child."*

# Stay-at-Home Mothers Have More Time to Raise Children

## Jennifer Roback Morse

*Dr. Jennifer Roback Morse is a mother and a columnist who taught economics for fifteen years at Yale and George Mason University. She is the author of* Love & Economics: Why the Laissez-Faire Family Doesn't Work, *from which the following viewpoint was taken. In it, the author describes how mothers who stay at home to personally raise their children are able to meet their individual needs in a way that paid childcare workers—either in the home or in group day-care settings—cannot do, whether from a lack of time, interest, or long-term commitment.*

As you read, consider the following questions:

1. In what ways is group childcare insufficient for infants?
2. According to advocates of paid childcare, what advantages does paid childcare offer?
3. According to the author, what advantages do parents have over professional caretakers when it comes to raising their children?

Some professional women think it an admission of weakness or defeat to acknowledge that they enjoy taking care of children. We are supposed to believe that child-care is mind-numbing, spirit-killing drudgery, and only work outside the home is fulfilling. These are not reasons for labor force participation that women would come up with spontaneously in the absence of any feminist tutoring. For many feminists, the overwhelming argument in favor of women working is that women with paychecks are more powerful than women without any income of their own. Those of us who admire the free market as a social mechanism agree that dollar power is real power. Each individual with a dollar is just as powerful as any other individual with a dollar. We sometimes tend to agree with feminists that working outside the home empowers women.

We should not concede this premise too readily. We forget that dollar power is not the only kind of power. Losing control over what happens to one's children is, for many women, a devastating loss of power. Surrendering day-to-day contact with one's children, giving up the ability to influence their development and surely count as losses of power from the viewpoint of most parents, fathers and mothers alike. The power of an independent income is important for a person who plans to be financially independent but not nearly so important for a person in an ongoing relationship.

Finally, we know that the principle that the market will provide does not mean that every family can hire Mary Poppins to provide full-time care. Childcare can only be a rational choice if the cost is lower than the woman's own wages. For women of moderate income, the only way this can be accomplished is through economies of scale in childcare. Group care will necessarily be the market-provided solution for the vast majority of women of modest means.

## Will an Employee Be Committed to a Child?

Institutional substitutes for the father's paycheck do not meet the needs of the mother and her child, especially their relationship needs. Neither an employer nor a government agency has reason to be committed to the mother and child. The same can be said of a paid childcare provider.

The baby needs the paid mother substitute to be present and attentive to his needs. The adult must come when the child cries. The adult must make a good effort to figure out what the crying signifies. This can be an impossible task because sometimes babies cry for no apparent reason at all. The adult might try everything he can think of to console the child: offer food, change diapers, or rock the baby. When the crying finally stops, the adult might still be mystified as to what it was all about. In these situations perhaps more than any other, it is important that the adult be present. The caregiver cannot simply throw up his or her hands and say "I'm leaving. This is too hard." We sometimes observe the very sad state of affairs in which the childcare provider *is* more committed and more attentive to the child's well-being than the parents are. If she is, this is most likely because the parental commitment level is so low. The nanny or babysitter does not particularly have reason to be more committed.

But even the best of babysitters quits, changes jobs, or moves on. No mother can count on a paid childcare provider's being committed to her for the duration of her child's early years. It might happen, but there is absolutely no reason to count on it. The childcare provider might do a perfectly fine

| Number of Stay-at-Home Spouses by Race and Income 2003 (numbers in the thousands) | | | | |
|---|---|---|---|---|
| Race | Income Level | Number of Married Couples | Working Mothers | Stay-at Home Mothers |
| White, Non-Hispanic | Below Poverty Level | 700 | 272 | 221 |
| | At or Above Poverty Level | 15,321 | 11,403 | 3,272 |
| Black | Below Poverty Level | 176 | 77 | 56 |
| | At or Above Poverty Level | 1,701 | 1,443 | 176 |
| Asian | Below Poverty Level | 82 | 19 | 28 |
| | At or Above Poverty Level | 1,105 | 723 | 308 |
| Hispanic | Below Poverty Level | 719 | 200 | 361 |
| | At or Above Poverty Level | 3,137 | 2,040 | 912 |
| All Other Races | Below Poverty Level | 45 | 20 | 19 |
| | At or Above Poverty Level | 475 | 347 | 102 |
| Total | Below Poverty Level | 1,684 | 570 | 668 |
| | At or Above Poverty Level | 21,524 | 15,801 | 4,720 |

TAKEN FROM: U.S. Census Bureau, Table FG8: "Married Couple Family Groups with Children under 15, by Stay-at-Home Status of Both Spouses, and Race and Hispanic Origin/1 of the Reference Person: 2003." http://www.census.gov/population/www/socdemo/hh-fam/cps2003. html.

job with the child, but what mother really wants her child to attach to the babysitter instead of herself? I have known women who quit their jobs when their children started calling the nanny "mommy."

## Young Children Thrive at Home

I am aware, of course, that many people defend infant day-care as beneficial to children. But social science research disputes the claim that group care meets the social needs of infants. The need for contact with children the same age does not really emerge until the toddler years. Newborns do not need to interact with each other. Other infants are competitors for adult attentiveness. If infants need any contact with other children at all, most probably they need the doting attention of older siblings. Infants also "take in" quite a bit of information by watching the activity around them. Older brothers and sisters provide role models for talking, crawling up the stairs, walking, and eating with a spoon, among other activities. An infant in a day-care center is unlikely to receive the kind of rich and varied attentiveness that is possible inside a family.

## Personal Attention at Home

There is an irony to the following pair of facts. Modern families evidently have a preference for small families. One of the arguments against large families is that children in small families can receive more attention from their parents. On the other hand, modern families seem to have a preference for leaving their children in group care, sometimes at very early ages.

Very high quality day-care centers proudly announce that their child to adult ratio is four to one for children under two years old, ten to one for preschoolers, twenty to one for school-age children—and they accept infants as young as six weeks old. I have many friends who home school their children. Some of these families have as many as ten children. I cannot think of a single such family that has four children under the age of two, or ten preschool children, or twenty second graders. Yet professional families with one or two children routinely leave them in group care facilities in which such child-adult ratios are common. Children of large families at least have each other. Does anybody really think that children are better off with no siblings and no time in the home? We baby-boomer mothers and modern career women seem to be rather schizophrenic about this matter.

## A Mother's Many Responsibilities

There are inherent limits to how much responsibility and authority parents can delegate to the people they hire.... To illustrate, let me summarize my activity as a stay-at-home mom on any given day. How are the basic jobs of instruction, direction, and guidance to be done with any particular child? One of my children has such a tender conscience that she bursts into tears at the realization of having done something wrong. The other requires a small two-by-four to even get the message that he has done wrong and needs to apologize. One child plays every minor injury for maximum drama. The other child is so impervious to pain, and so resistant to accepting help, that if you hear a whimper out of him, you should call for an ambulance. And the subtleties of settling quarrels! Who really started the fight? It looks for all the world as if big brother pushed and shoved, but little sister can be an irresistible provocateur.

Then there is the job of providing encouragement, skating that fine line between managing the child's frustration by not asking too much too soon and making legitimate and necessary demands for improvement and advancement. I know these children are fully capable of persuading a stranger that they cannot do very much. On the other hand, there is no point in asking them to do something that is so far beyond their capacity that I might as well be asking them to solve a differential equation.

They need help in their social interactions with each other and the other children in the neighborhood. They need more than a generalized instruction to share and be pleasant. Sometimes they honestly do not understand how to do what they are supposed to do. They would like to persuade another child to play with them (on their own terms, of course), but they have no idea what to offer them or how to speak to them. Sometimes, they are sorely tempted to do or say something they know they are not supposed to do, but they cannot quite see how to stop themselves or how to manage the frustration inherent in controlling their impulses. The gap between what they want to do and what they are supposed to do is too broad for them to jump. They need some coaching not only for their actions but for their words and even their thoughts.

As the child gets a little older, helping him learn to manage his frustration is a more important objective than helping him find strategies to get his own way. "That toy belongs to him. He doesn't have to let you play with it." "You wouldn't like it if he took your toys." "Don't you have enough toys? You need to be satisfied with what you have." Knowing when a particular child is ready for a new level of self-restraint, knowing what level of abstraction he can grasp, knowing how much frustration he can tolerate and helping him move to a new level, all of these are part of the daily work of motherhood.

## Delegating Child Care

Now I ask: Who am I going to pay to do all this? How am I going to give instructions of sufficient detail to a babysitter? . . . Of course, there is nothing wrong with hiring some help. But it is not possible to completely delegate the innumerable tasks that go into raising any particular child. . . .

Much of this knowledge about the child's needs is tacit, difficult to articulate and specify. When is this particular child ready to learn this particular skill? How much frustration can this child tolerate in attempting to learn something new? This tacit knowledge sets a limit on how much care of their children parents can reasonably delegate to others. It is possible that one trusted babysitter or relative could have sufficient intuitive feel for the child's needs and personality. But often it is much easier for the adult to just do what the child wants rather than to take the time to teach a new skill. It takes very dedicated paid help to put up with the costs of time and frustration involved in teaching such skills. . . .

Advocates of paid childcare have made . . . audacious claims. Paid child care would relieve intelligent women from the drudgery of meeting the endless demands of small children. Paid childcare would release a tremendous amount of productive energy into the economy as these intelligent women enter the labor force. Children would learn to become independent of their mothers earlier rather than being smothered by overprotective, underemployed, frustrated mothers. Children would become better socialized by being among their peers at earlier ages. Paid childcare is not only an adequate substitute for parental care, it is actually superior to a mother's care. . . .

## Drawbacks to Professional Care

The cost of losing localized, individual knowledge possessed and used by the ordinary inarticulate parent is far more profound than simply an economy going bust. Paid childcare providers do not have the same interest in the child as the parents nor the same incentives to invest in learning about the child. The people who have the incentive and the interests, namely the parents, cannot invest the same amount of time in learning all the detailed particular things about the individual child if they are spending the majority of their waking hours away from the child. The child grows up unknown. The child's visible material needs may be met, but his deeper intangible needs may not be.

Those of us who accepted the arguments in favor of paid child care did not realize how much knowledge our mothers really needed as they raised us. We did not realize how much individualized attentiveness we actually had received and how difficult it would be to pay someone to give our children what we received. Our mothers discovered what we needed in the process of being in a relationship with us. They could not easily convey to strangers everything they knew, and everything they routinely, if inarticulately, used. We did not realize that our mother's help with homework blunted the impact of being in educational institutions not necessarily geared to our individual needs. We did not realize how much our parents and older siblings helped us work out difficulties in our relationships with school friends and neighborhood children. Those talks around the kitchen table, or in the car, or before bedtime gave us more than we realized, guidance that cannot easily be replaced by a nanny or a day-care worker. We did not realize how much we received from long-term relationships with our siblings, relationships that cannot be replicated by classmates in a school or day-care center.

# Periodical Bibliography

*The following articles have been selected to supplement thediverse views presented in this chapter.*

| | |
|---|---|
| Ryan T. Anderson | "'Beyond Gay Marriage,'" *Weekly Standard*, August 15, 2006. |
| Judith Davidoff | "No Wedding Bells: Why Banning Same-Sex Marriage Spells Disaster," *Progressive*, August 2006. |
| Thomas R. Eddlem | "Homogenizing Homosexuality: Using Techniques that Allow a Tiny Minority to Gain Power over a Complacent Majority, Homosexual Activists Are Leading Massachusetts (and America) Down into a Moral Abyss," *New American*, November 28, 2005. |
| Valerie Frankel | "The Two-Apartment Marriage," *O, The Oprah Magazine*, November 2004. |
| Terry Martin Hekker | "Should You Stop Working when You Have Kids?" *Cosmopolitan*, June 2006. |
| Norma Jarboe and Lesley Nash | "Flexible Working and the Equalities Review: Head to Head," *Personnel Today*, March 13, 2007. |
| Pamela Kruger | "Daycare: Harmful or Helpful? (Allison Clarke-Stewart, Interview)," *Child*, June–July 2005. |
| Lynn Olcott | "The Ballad of the Working Mother: As a Single Mom Working Full-Time, Not Only Am I Bringing Home the Bacon, I Have to Cook It, Too," *Newsweek*, October 30, 2006. |
| Dee Dee Risher | "Our Crazy Dance," *The Other Side*, May–June 2004. |
| Phil Riske | "Marriage Initiative Brings Gay Official to Phoenix," *Arizona Capitol Times*, April 1, 2006. |
| Debra Rosenberg and Pat Wingert | "First Comes Junior in a Baby Carriage: Four in Ten Kids Are Now Born to Unmarried Moms," *Newsweek*, December 4, 2006. |

OPPOSING
VIEWPOINTS®
SERIES

CHAPTER 2

# What Dilemmas Do Would-Be Parents Face?

# Chapter Preface

What makes a parent?

In 1978, the world's first "test-tube baby" was born. Louise Brown is the product of an egg and sperm that were taken from her parents' bodies, combined in a laboratory, and then implanted in her mother's uterus. It was the first successful pregnancy and birth of a human embryo fertilized outside the human body. Since then, more than three million babies have been born with this procedure.

In 1985, Mary Beth Whitehead contracted with the married couple William and Elizabeth Stern to become pregnant with William's sperm and to relinquish the child for a fee of $10,000. When the daughter, referred to by the media as "Baby M," was born the next year, Whitehead refused to give her up. A court eventually awarded custody to the genetic father and his wife and gave legal visitation rights to Whitehead, the genetic mother.

In 2003, Janet Jenkins and Lisa Miller formally dissolved their same-sex civil union, which had been formed in Vermont. They together had been raising a child, who was born to Miller in 2002 and who was 15 months old when the civil union ended. Miller took the child to Virginia. In 2004, a Vermont court awarded Jenkins legal visitation rights akin to those a divorced spouse might receive. That same year, Miller took the case to court in Virginia—a state that does not acknowledge same-sex civil unions—to deny Jenkins parental rights. Jenkins still considers herself a mother to that child.

In 2006, Bell, a dachshund dog living in Carlton, Oregon, adopted two kittens to rear alongside her own litter of puppies. Gabi, a pit bull from Kalikino, Russia, not only adopted kittens but nursed them without ever having had puppies of her own.

Again, what makes a parent?

The drive to procreate is a potent biological instinct. The desire to survive in some sense is subordinate to the desire to pass along genes to the next generation, thus ensuring the continuity of the species. In this context, the abundance of love that parents feel for their children and the fierceness with which they protect them is understood as a manifestation of the human desire to perpetuate one's own genes in the next generation gene pool. Yet parents (of many species) express love for and protect children with whom they share no genetic link and for whom there is no personal evolutionary reason to justify their expense of effort. Adults go to great lengths, in fact, to demonstrate that they are worthy and deserving of relationships with children and spend lots of time and money just to find children with whom to create a family.

Still, the genetic link is respected and protected legally and socially. Attitudes in the law and culture in the early 2000s tend towards the preservation of biological families. These assumptions often result in some children spending long periods of time in foster care until their own parents learn how to take care of them, instead of being given a permanent adoptive home. It means that sometimes unknowing biological fathers find themselves sued for back child-support payments a decade after a birth they never knew happened. It also means that sometimes adopted children, who love their family and would never dream of living elsewhere, embark on searches for their biological parents just to see who they are.

The authors in the following chapter provide some answers to the many questions that arise over the difficulties that face people who wish to become parents but cannot easily do so, and pose further questions about how parents find children, how families are artificially constructed, and how much biology matters.

*"Everyone in the fertility market, everyone in the adoption market, and everyone who purchases eggs, sperm, wombs, and PGD is looking for precisely the same thing: a child to call their own."*

# The Baby Market Should Be Regulated

*Debora L. Spar*

*Debora L. Spar is a professor, the senior associate dean, and the director of research at Harvard Business School; her primary interests are in government, business, and international trade. The following viewpoint appears in her book,* The Baby Business. *In the viewpoint, the author argues that family building through medicine and adoption really is a market for children and should be acknowledged as such. Only when society accepts that babies are for sale can it help create families fairly and efficiently.*

As you read, consider the following questions:

1. Why does the author say that infertility doctors and adoption social workers perform the same function?

Debora L. Spar, "Songs of Solomon," *The Baby Business: How Money, Science, and Politics Drive the Commerce of Conception.* Boston, MA: Harvard Business School Press, 2006, pp. 195–233. Copyright © 2006 Harvard Business School Publishing Corporation. Reproduced by permission.

2. What are some examples of how the costs and services in the unregulated baby market vary from state to state and from consumer to consumer?

3. What are the most likely social and economic outcomes if the baby market remains unregulated?

Say the word *market,* and what comes to mind? Financial markets, maybe, or supermarkets. There are markets in real estate; markets in used cars; markets filled with farmers selling pumpkins and cheese. There are markets in odd things like used Pez dispensers and in highly sophisticated instruments like mortgage-backed securities. But babies? Babies aren't supposed to be sold. Babies aren't supposed to be bought. Babies aren't supposed to have prices fixed on them. . . .

Yet . . . the market for babies—the market for children, really—is still a market. How do we know? It's because there is a deep and persistent demand for reproduction, a demand that often goes far beyond what nature alone can provide. There is supply in this market, too, a wide and steadily increasing supply of ways to produce when procreation fails. There are prices that clearly link supply and demand, and there are businesses that sell their wares in this market, often charging hefty sums along the way. . . .

## A Market Full of Variances

Adoption, fertility treatment, surrogacy, even genetic engineering—they are all intimately connected to one another and to the promise they offer of providing children for those who desire them. If the ultimate demand is for a child to raise, then each of the baby markets can be seen as a substitute of sorts, with parents choosing among the types of production they prefer and the kinds of risk they are willing to accept. . . .

Currently [as of 2006], . . . the various baby markets exist as almost completely separate entities. Fertility treatments are the province of specialized clinics and medical experts, of endocrinologists and embryologists who are frequently attached to large university hospitals. When prospective parents go to fertility clinics, they present themselves as patients: they have a medical problem and are seeking a medical solution. The fertility specialists then treat them accordingly, doing whatever they can to fix the underlying physical problem and, eventually, to produce a child.

Note, however, that the *child* is not really the focus in this part of the baby trade; instead, it is the would-be parents' infertility. During the course of fertility treatment, therefore, doctors do not typically suggest alternatives to their own form of treatment; they rarely advise their patients to contemplate adoption, foster care, or living without children. Such options simply are not within the confines of their profession: even though they are actually in the business of providing children for parents to raise, they define their role as curing infertility. They are medical experts performing a particular form of health care. As one doctor explains, "We don't sell babies. We sell care of the infertile couple. We sell a process, not an outcome."

Meanwhile, suppliers to the infertility trade function much like suppliers in other, less intimate realms. Hormone producers, for example, are simply pharmaceutical firms, providing highly valued inputs without much downward pressure on price. They invest in R&D [research and development], patent their drugs, and sell directly to fertility specialists. They sell products rather than services and have a well-established system of property rights. Egg and sperm "producers" are very different, of course: they are individuals rather than firms and produce only small (for eggs) or limited (for sperm) amounts of product. Yet they are still producers and are essentially treated as such in the market. They aren't medical practitioners; they aren't providing children; they don't directly cure infertility. Instead, like the hormone manufacturers, they produce a tangible product that is subsequently sold into the baby business.

## The Market Becomes Even More Complicated

Wombs are more complicated, because they are typically leased rather than sold. Surrogate mothers provide a service instead of a product and retain a more complicated relationship with the children they bear. Unlike egg or sperm donors, surrogates aren't really producers, but neither are they birth mothers in the typical sense of adoption. Specialists who perform PGD [pre-implantation genetic diagnosis] are also complicated, because they provide medical services that are linked to infertility but not directly connected to it. Essentially, these doctors produce healthy children rather than fertile parents.

And then there is adoption, which sits oddly apart from the rest of the baby trade. In adoption, the child is much more tangible than in any of the other, related markets. In adoption, the child is real rather than potential, fully formed rather than composed of disparate parts. In adoption, the child has a pre-existing set of parents and a visible or detectable set of traits. Providers in the adoption market, therefore, function very differently from their counterparts in the fertility trade. They are social workers, not doctors, and they are charged, at least in theory, with focusing on the existing child rather than the prospective parent. As a result, they are less overtly commercial and more frequently nonprofit. Most importantly, they are required, often explicitly, to divorce their activities from those of the fertility trade. Although many parents arrive at adoption after suffering from infertility, adoption agencies insist that these parents not see adoption as a "cure" for infertility. They insist, in other words, in splitting adoption from fertility treatment, just as fertility clinics resolutely avoid the topic of adoption.

Yet in reality these two markets are closely linked. Many people pursue fertility treatment because they are wary of adoption. Many others pursue adoption because they have grown weary of or dissatisfied with fertility treatment. Both sides of this market would prefer to believe that they are not substitutes for one another. But in reality, of course, they are. Everyone in the fertility market, everyone in the adoption market, and everyone who purchases eggs, sperm, wombs, and PGD is looking for precisely the same thing: a child to call their own.

## Regulation Promotes Consistency

Typically, markets that sell similar goods are subjected to similar regulatory regimes. Under U.S. law, pumpkins, for example, are treated much like squash or rutabagas. Home heating oil is governed by the same rules as natural gas. And the market for knee replacements works just like the market for hip replacements. In each of these cases, the kind of regulation and the level of regulation don't vary much. So if pumpkin farmers are subject to the basic rules of fair play and safe practice—not to use certain pesticides, for example, nor to employ slave labor—a similar set of rules is likely to apply to farmers producing squash and rutabagas. If prices are capped for home heating oil, they will almost certainly be capped for natural gas as well. . . .

These regulatory consistencies are a hallmark of modern economies. Yet in the baby business, they simply do not apply. Instead, as noted earlier, each of the segments in this market functions separately, and each is subject to its own idiosyncratic set of rules.

To understand the depth of these differences, it is useful to consider the examples set out in [the accompanying] table. Sperm, as we see, is subject to only a hint of regulation: under FDA [Food and Drug Administration] guidelines, sperm banks must be certified by a federal agency and must comply with certain quality control provisions. Eggs, by contrast, are subject to a vaguer set of rules, because it's not entirely clear whether, or under what conditions, the FDA regards them as "reproductive tissues." . . .

Adding price to this picture makes it even more complicated, because prices vary both in nominal terms and in the amount of reimbursement available. For example, the "price" of pregnancy for most Americans is essentially nothing. Pregnant women receive prenatal care, spend time in the hospital, and deliver their babies—all, usually, without paying the full cost of the services they have received. This isn't, of course, because these services are free—indeed, the typical costs of a normal pregnancy run between $7,000 and $12,000—but because we, as a society, have decided to spread these costs more widely. Thus, most insurance companies are required by law to cover the costs of pregnancy. . . .

The price of an assisted pregnancy is much higher, even though it arguably leads to precisely the same result: the birth of a child for its parents to raise. What is even more interesting, though, is that the various technical routes to this result are themselves priced so disparately. Eggs run the gamut from $3,000 to $50,000, and surrogates from $10,000 to $75,000. IVF is fully covered in some states, partially covered in others, and left entirely to the free market in most. . . .

One could argue, of course, that such variation is not necessarily bad. There are other markets—think of wine, for example, or land—where prices vary even more and states also impose different regulatory regimes. But babies, obviously, are different. Because as a society we value babies more than wine or land. We treat them, not as rights per se, but at least as something to which all citizens have a nearly identical claim. How, then, can we say that some people can procreate for free, whereas others must pay? And how can we permit such significant variation across state lines and between different versions of assisted procreation? . . .

**Some Regulatory Variances in the Baby Market**

| Component | Federal regulation | State regulation | | | |
|---|---|---|---|---|---|
| | | *Massachusetts* | *California* | *Florida* | *North Dakota* |
| Sperm | Banks subject to FDA regulation as "clinical laboratories" | Donation permitted; consenting husband is legal father | Donation permitted; consenting husband is legal father | Donation permitted; consenting husband is legal father | Donation permitted; consenting husband is legal father |
| Eggs | Subject, under some conditions, to FDA regulation as "clinical laboratories" | No law; donation permitted | No law; donation permitted | Donation permitted; reasonable compensation allowed | Donation permitted; law says donor is not the parent of the child |
| IVF | Clinics must report success rates to CDC | Permitted; insurance must cover costs of IVF | Permitted; insurance may exclude costs of IVF | Permitted; insurance must offer *option* of IVF coverage | Permitted; no requirements for insurance coverage |
| Surrogacy | No law | No law | No law; court decisions in favor of "intended" parents | Law presumes that contracting couple are legal parents; payment prohibited | Contract void; surrogate and her husband are legal parents |
| Adoption | Entry of foreign-born children subject to State Department rules; placement of foster children subject to national law | No independent adoption | Independent adoption, advertising, and reimbursement permitted | Independent adoption, advertising, and reimbursement permitted | Independent adoption permitted; advertisement only by state or licensed agency |

TAKEN FROM: Debora L. Spar, *The Baby Business*, p. 212, 2006.

## Treat All Facets of the Baby Business as One

A broad overview of the baby business, therefore, shows a landscape marked by variance. Similar clients find themselves in vastly different markets, depending on where they live and how they choose to pursue a child. Theoretically, these markets can be defined as wholly separate entities: the market for orphaned girls in China, after all, is very different from the market for IVF [in vitro fertilization] in Milwaukee. But in practice they are intimately connected, because the little girl in China is at some level a direct substitute for the baby that might be produced via IVF.

We have chosen by default to keep these markets separate, but that is not the only alternative. Indeed, another option— and a far better one—would be to acknowledge the various facets of the baby business as part of a broader whole and then to conceive of the market, and regulate the market, as one. . . .

## Regulation: The Best of Four Options

Demand in the baby business is not likely to diminish any time soon. On the contrary, changing demographics and social mores, combined with exploding technological prospects, suggest that increasing numbers of people will want to exert control over conception. They will want to control when they conceive, how they conceive, and even, increasingly, the characteristics of the children they raise as their own. Unless we want this market to explode out of control, we as a society have only four viable options.

The first option is to leave the baby business to the normal course of market forces, allowing supply and demand alone to determine the shape of this trade. Under this structure, supply will flourish but only the rich will enjoy its benefits. At the extreme, such a course leads to the grisly future painted by critics such as Francis Fukuyama, who fears a world populated eventually by two subspecies: the GenRich and the GenPoor.

Following that line of reasoning, we could, alternatively, choose to ban the baby business, deciding that its risks and inherent inequities are simply too great. Yet . . . prohibition at this point seems futile: demand in the baby business is simply too high and the technologies too good.

And so we could choose a third option, treating high-technology reproduction like organ transplants and removing exchange completely from the market. This alternative is more feasible than the first two and is already, to some extent, the operative model in adoption. Again, though, history suggests that expanding this model to the farther reaches of the baby trade would be exceedingly difficult. The supply (of eggs, sperm, wombs, and embryos) is already available and the players in place.

Which leaves us, really, with only one option. If we don't want the baby business left fully to either the state or the market, we need to find a way of splitting the difference. We need, in other words, to regulate it. . . .

It's no use being coy about the baby market or cloaking it in fairy-tale prose. We are making babies now, for better or worse, in a very high-tech way. We are procuring these babies from a wide array of sources, and we are pushing deeper into the components of their birth. We can moralize about these developments if we desire, ruing the gods who pushed nature aside. We can decry the fate of our manipulated offspring, closing our eyes and trying to make them fade back in time. Or we can plunge into the market that desire has created, imagining how we can shape our children and secure our children without destroying ourselves.

> "Some agencies circulate a fee schedule
> with children listed in categories by race
> and sex with prices proportionate to
> their disability."

# Children Should Not
# Be Bought and Sold

*Darlene Gerow*

*Darlene Gerow is the editor of* The CUB Communicator, *the
newsletter of Concerned United Birthparents (CUB). CUB is an
organization that serves all people affected by adoption, especially parents who have given up their children to adoption. In
the following viewpoint, the author makes the case that the demand for infants to adopt far exceeds the supply of infants that
need homes, which has caused adoption programs to become
thinly disguised markets and adoption agencies to aggressively
persuade women to give up their babies.*

As you read, consider the following questions:

1. Why are there fewer children available for adoption now
   than in previous decades?

2. How do most parents who relinquish their children to adoption today differ from the traditional image of mothers who do so?

3. In what ways do "baby dump" laws serve the interests of adoption agencies and political adoption lobbies?

A doption is perceived by society as primarily an altruistic act where a child is rescued from a dreadful fate. The child's mother is portrayed as not wanting her child and the child's father as usually being nonexistent. The adopting parents are mythically portrayed as saint-like rescuers who provide a "happily ever after." In reality, birthparents anguish over the loss of their children, adoptive families are just as dysfunctional as natural families, and adoption is a huge, profit-driven industry where babies are the commodity. As it is currently [as of 2002] practiced in America, infant adoption by non-relatives does more to meet the needs of affluent adopters than to help children.

## Billion Dollar U.S. Industry

Infant adoption is big business in America. Approximately 140,000 adoptions are finalized each year although it remains unclear how many are infant adoptions and how many are older children adopted by relatives or foster parents. According to an industry analysis by Marketdata Enterprises, Inc. of Tampa, Florida, adoption provider revenues in 2000 were $1.44 billion with a projected industry annual growth rate of 11.5 percent to 2004.

Ken Watson, named the 1992 Child Advocate of the Year by the North American Council on Adoptable Children, explains that the outright sale of children is illegal, but adopters are routinely charged fees to legally parent a child. Watson recounts how some agencies circulate a fee schedule with children listed in categories by race and sex with prices proportionate to their desirability. Prices can range from $25,000 to

$50,000 and upwards. According to Watson, although adoption providers insist that the fee is not payment for a child, but rather money to cover the cost of services provided, "Adoptive parents are not deceived. They know they are paying for a child." Adopters with the most money obtain the children considered the most desirable.

Along with the fees charged by the adoption provider, adopters routinely reimburse relinquishing parents for expenses incurred during the pregnancy. Although these expenses are paid as an act of charity and are not tax deductible, there are adoption facilitators and Web site sources that coach adopters as to how much they dare pay a relinquishing mother for such things as cars, clothes, and tuition without crossing the line into baby buying.

James Gritter, open adoption practitioner with Catholic Human Services, Inc., observes, "Birthfamilies are ostensibly given money to make their experience more tolerable, but the 'relief' they receive may soon feel like blood money, ultimately producing unspeakable guilt and misery." Gritter explains that reimbursement for expenses is coercive because when adopters invest in prospective birthparents, they expect a return on their investment. The money a young mother receives during her pregnancy is coercive because it may cause her to feel indebted to the adopters and prevent her from following her heart after birth and parenting her own baby.

## Baby Selling?

Since the business of adoption has become so lucrative, it has attracted many professionals never previously interested in adoption. In the last ten years, the number of attorneys involved in adoption has doubled. Gritter contends that adoption has changed from "a professional model, in which service providers hang out their shingles and aspire to suspend self-interest, to a business model that aggressively recruits consumers on a buyer-beware basis." Randolph W. Severson, director of Heart Words: an Adoptee Advocacy and Counseling Center, cautions, "The trend runs perilously close to that cliff called selling babies."

One of the more outrageous examples of the excesses surfacing in the adoption industry appeared recently [as of 2002] in *Talk* magazine in an article by Jim DeFede. DeFede reports on a boutique adoption service in Florida and its elite baby broker, Richard Gitelman, who places ads nationally seeking pregnant women, and then auctions their babies to the highest bidder among the adopters on his list. His prices vary from $75,000 to $250,000 for healthy white infants. Increasingly, for-profit businesses and unlicensed facilitators promise to connect prospective adopters with the child of their dreams and charge whatever the market will bear.

## Competition for Infants

There is a huge disparity in the supply-and-demand of infants, which creates desperate and intense competition among adopters. Currently [as of 2002], there are forty or more adopters vying for every healthy white infant that becomes available for adoption. There are fewer desirable adoptable infants because society has become more accepting of single mothers who parent their children than in the past. The stigma of bearing a child out-of-wedlock has diminished, so the vast majority of today's single mothers choose to keep their babies instead of relinquishing them to adoption. Effective birth control methods are readily available to the fertile population, and, since abortion is legal, an unplanned pregnancy can be terminated.

While the supply of desirable adoptable infants has been decreasing, infertility in America has been increasing. It is estimated that one in six couples has trouble conceiving and that there may be as many as 5.3 million infertile couples in America. Many adopters who are currently seeking babies postponed child bearing to pursue their careers, and, later, when they finally wanted to conceive, found that due to age they were infertile. Unrelated to age, another cause of infertility is chlamydia. Dubbed the "silent epidemic," chlamydia is the most frequently reported infectious disease in the U.S. and often results in infertility because there are few symptoms. Many people do not realize they were ever infected with chlamydia until they later discover complications, such as infertility.

Although adoption does not cure infertility, and adopting a child is not the same as having a child by birth, many of the infertile eventually pursue adopting a baby. In *U.S. News & World Report*, Clark and Shute relate that the majority of adopters want only healthy infants because most foster children awaiting homes are at least five years old, many have physical or emotional handicaps, and most are of mixed races.

## A Scarce and Dear Commodity

With such market demand, the adoption industry is striving to increase the supply of desirable adoptable babies. Historian Rickie Solinger writes in *Beggars and Choosers: How the Politics of Choice Shapes Adoption, Abortion and Welfare in the United States* that Representative Pat Schroeder of Colorado claims there are too many single women in the U.S. having babies with too few of them giving up their babies for adoption. Schroeder labeled babies "a scarce and dear commodity." Representative Schroeder supports the adoption industry and does not see anything wrong with viewing babies as a resource to meet the needs of adults.

Domestically, efforts are underway to encourage women to relinquish their babies for adoption; however, it is the rare mother who actually wants to be separated from her child. According to the twenty-five year old national organization, Concerned United Birthparents, Inc., mothers surrender their babies due to a lack of financial resources, lack of extended family support, and pressure by social workers or other adoption facilitators. Mothers who have relinquished their children grieve for the remainder of their lives. Losing a child, whether to death or to adoption, is a tragedy from which a mother never completely recovers. Her relinquished child never recovers from the separation either.

Traditionally, most babies relinquished for adoption were born to single, unwed, teenage mothers, but that is no longer the case. According to long-time adoption reformist and co-author of *The Adoption Triangle*, Reuben Pannor, more than half of the babies relinquished today are born to impoverished married couples in the Bible Belt and other areas with high rates of poverty. Most currently, relinquishing families already have two or more children who are the brothers and sisters of the relinquished baby. Pannor explains, "These birthparents come from the poverty pockets of our country and are the primary targets of attorneys who flood their communities with enticing advertisements."

Adoptive mother Ruth Reichl's recent article in *More* tells how at thirty-nine years old she had undergone extensive infertility treatments when her doctor admitted defeat and suggested that she consider adopting. Her doctor recommended an attorney who was "sleek and handsome" and to whom "[...] the adoption industry had clearly been good." The attorney explained that he would target "pregnant southern women who lacked either the means or the desire to raise their babies."

Poor women are especially vulnerable to the high-pressured tactics of the adoption industry. Without resources or support, they want to believe that their sacrifice really will be helpful to their children. Rarely are they informed about the long-term repercussions they and their children will experience as a result of separation.

# Descriptions of Children Available for Adoption

(GUATEMALA FEMALE)

Dulce was born in Guatemala and is living with a foster family there. She is healthy and tested negative to HIV, Hep-B and VDRL. Her weight is 6.1 lbs and her height is 48.1 cms with a cc of 32.8 cms. Her birth mother is 25 years old and also tested negative to HIV 1&2.

(LATIN AMERICA MALE)

This beautiful baby boy was born just three days ago. He has not been named so the adoptive parents will be allow to name him. His medical reports state he is healthy and his mother's lab work came back negative. He was born without complications and weighed 9 lbs at birth.

(ASIA)

This beautiful baby boy has a sweet and gentle manner. He is described by his caregivers as smart and bright with quick reflexes. His favorite thing to do is to be taken outdoors. Jun also likes to play games and imitate others. He especially likes to play with his toys, and is very attached to his favorite stuffed elephant. His caregivers love him very much and say that little Jun is a very sweet child.

(AFRICA OLDER SIBLINGS)

Here is another attractive sibling set. Elder sister is 10 years old and was born on August 19, 1996 and younger brother is 8 years old born on August 4, 1998. Their bio mother died of cancer in June of 2003 and father is unemployed and unable to meet their basic needs. He is hopeful for them to be adopted and have an opportunity for a brighter future.

Rainbowkids: *The International Adoption E-Magazine, 2007,*
*www.rainbowkids.com.*

## Industry Promotes Relinquishment

In order to promote adoption and encourage the relinquishment of infants, the adoption industry employs full-time lobbyists in Washington, D.C. The National Council for Adoption is a private lobbying group whose members include twenty-eight adoption agencies and represents 3.5 percent of U.S. adoption agencies. The N.C.F.A. and three adoption agencies just received $8.6 million from the federal treasury in October 2001 to promote adoption to pregnant women at health centers and clinics. In the press release from the U.S.A. Department of Health and Human Services, Tommy G. Thompson, H.H.S. secretary, said, "These grants are an important step in making sure that every pregnant woman who is considering her alternatives understands the benefits of adoption."

Relinquishment and adoption is considered by some to be a solution for the societal problem of illegitimacy and welfare dependency. Psychologist Lynne Reyman contends that by viewing adoption as a cure for poverty, we deny the humanity of birthparents. By taking the children of poor families, we compound their problems; not only are they still poor, but additionally they have lost their children.

## The Industry Tightens the Screws

Other lobbying and legislative efforts of the adoption industry include supporting states to legally reduce the length of time after which relinquishment becomes irrevocable. California recently reduced the time a relinquishing mother has to change her mind from ninety to thirty days.

Some states allow no time for reconsideration. Some states have enacted legislation that allows the mother to sign a binding relinquishment even before her baby is born. Before birth, a pregnant woman may think relinquishment is the best solution for her predicament. Following birth, once the mother actually meets her infant, her priorities often change drastically. A mother needs to experience motherhood and understand the full implications of relinquishment before she signs anything.

The adoption industry aggressively supports both anti-abortion legislation and the recent "baby dump" laws. Thirty-five states have passed safe haven laws in the last two years [2000 to 2002]. These laws allow anyone to anonymously abandon a baby at a designated safe place. Ostensibly, their intent is to reduce infanticide, but inadvertently they encourage and condone the abandonment of infants. Since the surrender is anonymous, there are no safeguards against fraud and corruption. There is no way to confirm that the person dumping the baby is the parent or legal guardian or if both parents have agreed to the abandonment. The "baby dump" laws are supported by the adoption lobby, who see the foundlings as a source of infants for adoption.

The Internet has become the tool of choice for adopters seeking pregnant women who might consider relinquishing their babies. Laura Mansnerus reported in the *New York Times* that hopeful adopters typically pay $175 to be listed in an Internet registry for three months. Their profiles in the registry include photos, family histories, and loving descriptions of their homes, pets, hobbies, and child-rearing plans. The Internet allows adopters to advertise for babies, which is illegal in other mediums in some states.

## Professional Marketing

"Public relations and marketing firms with very bright and likeable marketing experts have orchestrated the commercial approach to adoption, and in their effort to make relinquishment and adoption appeal to pregnant women, they have disguised the process to make it appear as though it prioritizes birthparents," Gritter explains. Watson describes the phenomena as having "spawned a host of ancillary exploiters, including public relations and marketing firms that help prospective adoptive parents prepare biographies and photographs to increase their appeal [. . .] and insurance companies who will write a policy to reimburse [prospective] adoptive parents who have paid the expenses of a [prospective] birthparent who then decides against adoption."

The National Adoption Network was one of the first national organizations dedicated to connecting pregnant women with adopters. Severson recounts how Dian Jordan brought her skills as an advertising executive to the National Adoption Network and employed high-gloss polished creativity to solicit prospective birthparents. . . .

## A Perfect World

The business of infant adoption is out of control. The affluent can buy any commodity they desire, including babies, while at the same time, poverty is the leading cause of relinquishment. Describing a perfect world where no babies would ever be relinquished for adoption, Barbara Eck Manning, founder of Resolve, an organization for infertile people, explains that the fact that babies are available reflects society's failure to provide education, family planning, medical services and support for at-risk families. Every adoption represents a tragic breakdown of a family where a mother and child have been separated.

*"Adoption is a negative, punitive exercise of robbing babies and children from their mothers, their heritage, their roots, their identities, and their rights as human beings."*

# Adoption Hurts Children

*Anne Patterson*

*Anne Patterson is an author, adopted person, and licensed private investigator with a 95.4 percent success rate in reuniting families separated by adoption. The following viewpoint directly addresses people who are considering giving up a baby for adoption and urges them to consider the negative effects of this action before making any decisions. The author points out that adoption is a permanent solution to what is usually a temporary problem and suggests that both the adopted-out infant and the relinquishing parent will suffer for the rest of their lives from their mutual separation and loss.*

As you read, consider the following questions:

1. What connections have newborn infants already made with their natural mothers?

Anne Patterson, "Dear Birthparent: What the Baby Brokers Don't Tell You about Adoptees and the Truth!" *www.keepyourbaby.com*, 2001. Copyright © 2001 Anne Patterson. Reproduced by permission of the author.

2. In what ways does Patterson say that adoption creates lies and illusions?

3. What two myths do "baby brokers" promulgate about natural mothers?

For all the things that are written and told about adoption, few are the truth. As a reunited adult adoptee I hope to shed as much light on this issue as possible within my lifetime.

If asked by anyone considering adoption "Is adoption a good choice?" My answer unreservedly would be "No". Adoption is NOT a healthy or a good choice. *If you ask a baby if they want to be adopted they would say, if they could talk a thousand times over, "NO"*. Each year hundreds of people are lied to about adoption, it is time for those who are its experts to come forward and share its reality.

Adoption is a permanent solution to a temporary situation. It is important to stress that it is NOT the baby that is a problem, it is the circumstances in one's life that is or could be presently challenging.

*Adoption is a negative, punitive exercise of robbing babies and children from their mothers, their heritage, their roots, their identities, and their rights as human beings.* Adoptees lose from the minute they are separated from their mothers. This loss is cloaked in lies and illusions.

## The Natural Connection between Babies and Mothers

For those promoting adoption, the idea is that it is a gain for the baby or the child. Being surrendered for adoption is not a gain in the least. No amount of money, or a two-parent family, or anything can replace the real and natural mother for adoptees. Nothing can replace the heritage and connections with others in the natural family as well. They won't tell you this but I will—from day one we grieve and are sad to have lost our mothers and are not happy! Not only are babies sad, they are also afraid. *We know our mothers, we grow inside their wombs. We hear the music of their hearts, we know their smell, we trust and love them by nature. They are ours, our universe—* all that we know, all that we feel, love and are attached to. Adoption takes our universe away. If someone took away all that you love and all that you know how would you feel?

*When we are born we only want one thing: to be held and loved by our own mothers. We know them, they belong to us and us to them.* To take that away is not good for babies. It is the worst most abusive act emotionally to inflict. When adoptees lose their mothers they lose themselves as well. They forever lose the person that they were born to be, and they lose the joy and right of being that person.

Above all we lose trust from the very beginning of the separation. The loss of trust is not a temporary feeling that is lessened by being adopted. That is another famous lie promoted by baby brokers. It is forever and permanent just like adoption is.

## A Lesson of Loss

*When the first lesson in life is that the one person you love and trust will go away, it is hardly a good start for anyone.* Along with the broken trust is grief and sorrow. This is not a lesson . . . to inflict on helpless infants. Being severed from your mother and family is not anything that adoptees are happy about. The loss in adoption for adoptees can rarely ever be expressed or acknowledged. There is a horrible expectation and false belief that the adopters and adoption will overcome any damage done to adoptees. This is another lie—it cannot undo our pain in losing our real families. In fact it makes the pain worse as it is so often denied to begin with. The truth is that we are traumatized from the separation and always will be. The grief that we feel as infants is not ever acknowledged. This lack of support also breaks our trust. It also makes us untrusting of our own feelings when our first feelings are bla-tantly ignored. It is normal for babies to be sad and in grief when they lose their mothers—what is NOT NORMAL IS ADOPTION to begin with.

Anyone considering adoption should know and see them-selves as having value and worth. Above all they should know that they are NOT replaceable. Babies are not interchangeable entities to be adopted without negative effects either. In truth, the bonds of nature are not replaceable any more than the mother or the baby is to begin with!

## Another Hard Lesson

*Along with the broken trust and the grief, the second lesson in life for adoptees is to be fake and live in worlds of illusions.* From the minute of the adoption [they] are conditioned to be someone else.

Adoptees are forced to take on the identity of strangers. We are not born to adopters, social workers or social agencies. We are born to two parents. Our birth certificates are falsified, then locked away. Our grief is not locked away though! Adop-tion changes our names; it cannot change either a baby's or a mother's heart or the lifelong loss that both will forever expe-rience.

*One of the arguments for adoption is that adoptees will gain two parents. This is ridiculous as we already have them.* This is the first lie used to coerce people considering adoption. If you are pregnant and reading this know reality—you are the baby's mother not anyone else. The baby also has a father. The father may be unsupportive or supportive but the reality is your baby has two parents to start with.

Our personalities and our lives are assumed to be shaped to those of our adopters. The famous lie [is] we will be just like them. Babies are born with set personalities, genes, behav-iors, temperaments, likes and dislikes. This is not an idea; it is a FACT! The idea of shaping a baby that is already a human

## A Child's Letter to Her Birth Mother

When I first went to my new mommy, I missed you—your heartbeat, the sound of your voice. But I learned to love my new parents. They made me feel special, and they told me how they had chosen me. Then, when I went to school and told the story to a friend, she asked why *you* didn't choose me. I didn't know the answer. I felt so helpless, so I just got angry.

*"A Child's Letter to Her Birth Mother."* Focus on Your Child, *2005, www.focusonyoungchild.com.*

being with a personality is again not healthy; it is negative. For adoptees fitting into another person's life at the expense of not being themselves—does not foster self-esteem or happiness. It breeds only one thing—insecurity, self-doubt and fear. It is not natural to live with strangers and pretend to be born to them. It is not fair, and it is not in the best interests of anyone other than adopters. It denies babies and children their rights to be only one thing—exactly who they were born to be.

## The Lifelong Impact of Lies

This continual lying that adoptees must live with manifests itself in thousands of ways. Adoptees are sad to be adopted, angry and insecure. The myth of the happy, grateful adoptee is nothing more than a blatant fantasy spread by baby brokers, and adopters. . . .

The denial of our real selves causes irreparable harm and again breaks trust! This is not in our best interests or any child's, for that matter.

For adoptees, being adopted does not feel like love or happiness. It feels as though we are unloved. It feels like we are unwanted, not good enough and not quite right. These feelings are not just light feelings that adoptees experience for a short time. They are life-long, deep and permanent. They cause permanent scars that do not go away.

## Nature Trumps Nurture

We have genetic influences that are strong, and in fact stronger than nurture to start with. Babies and children will NOT BE JUST LIKE ADOPTERS. They will in fact favor and be like their real parents. Above all why should we be just like strangers, we are not their children; we are the children of our real parents. All children should have the right to love and be proud of themselves, and to love and be proud of who they are. *Adoption turns pride into shame, love into fear, and robs children of their right to be happy as they are.*

For many promoting adoption, the idea of income and wealth for the child may sound appealing. Fancy houses, cars and trips around the world is a shallow way to look at life. Life is not about money. It is much deeper than that. The poorest of children if loved will be rich in the ways that count. Adoption for material gain is wrong. Material possessions and financial opportunities do NOT replace a baby's or a child's desire to love and be parented by their own parents. NO AMOUNT of money in a child's life is worth it to be separated from their real parents. Better to be poorer and loved by your own than to be richer and live with lies, secrets, illusions and sorrow.

## Myths about Mothers

Another despicable myth is that the natural mother will be sentenced to poverty forever. This is a condescending and ridiculous lie. Having worked with hundreds of natural mothers I can attest to the fact that the average first mother was not . . . the starving street person that baby brokers have lied about for years! A person may well be having some financial difficulty and may well be worried of providing for a child at some point in their lives. Finances can change. Jobs are available, training and education are both available, other alternatives are available! While a person's finances can change adoption cannot. Again it is a permanent solution that will not change! If you are considering adoption due to a temporary financial situation, then please think of this as being exactly that—"temporary". I believe humans are more than capable of productive and healthy changes. Everyone can learn new things and grow. One's situation now can always change—adoption can NOT!

Yet another argument used to promote adoption is the question of youth. *Being young is not a bad thing; it is [not] negative and it is not dangerous. Young people can be excellent caregivers and parents.* For those that wish to support adoption and promote it—this is yet another thing that they manipulate and lie about. It is as if the young person will be young forever. They will always be sixteen or seventeen or the age at the time of pregnancy. Just as babies grow so do teenagers, so do adults. You will not be young forever. You will mature and you will grow. It is more than possible to learn how to parent at a young age. The baby brokers will convince you that it is not—will you believe them or will you believe yourself? Above all will you believe in the lives of strangers or the lives of you and your baby as being more than possible to be happy and healthy?

You can grow with your baby, learn new things and parent a child at a young age. There is a myriad of resources to help young people with parenting. Babies living with older strangers is hardly in their best interests. Being older is not and does not mean better than a young mother or father, period. Always remember you will not be young forever! It will not matter to your baby if you are young, as your baby will love you regardless of age. . . .

Finally, I would like to ask anyone considering adoption one thing: If you were surrendered for adoption and you lost your most beloved person—your real mother? If you were forced to deny that the loss hurt you and pretend that it did not? If you were forced to live with strangers. If you were forced to be someone that you were not. If your life was a lie and you were forced to be part of a family that you are not a part of. If your identity was hidden from you. If your identity was lied about by everyone in your life. If you were forbidden to know your real name, see your real family, know your real life—would you be happy or grateful? Likely not.

| "Adoption needs to be embraced, not as
a punishment for unfit parents, but as
a gift of loving for the child."

# Adoption Helps Children

## Janet Albrechtsen

*Janet Albrechtsen is a columnist, commentator, former lawyer,
and a board member of the non-profit Australian Broadcasting
Company. In the following viewpoint, the author laments the
view of adoption as a strategy of last resort to be avoided if at
all possible in favor of reuniting severely dysfunctional families.
The author argues that children—especially the tens of thousands bouncing between foster homes and institutions in Australia—deserve permanent love and stability far more than their
abusive or neglectful parents deserve multiple chances to rehabilitate and regain custody at the expense of their children's well-
being.*

As you read, consider the following questions:

1. What was the philosophy and ultimate goal of
   Australia's 2002 child welfare system?
2. By what comparisons should the success of an adoption
   and the outcome for an adopted child be judged?

Janet Albrechtsen, "Restoring Adoption," *Quadrant*, vol. 46, January–February 2002,
pp. 15–19. Copyright © 2002 Quadrant Magazine Company, Inc. Reproduced by permission of the publisher and author.

3. What reasons do anti-adoption groups give for their objections to separating biological parents and children?

An empty cradle sits in the middle of the cobbled courtyard of a grand old building on Madison Avenue in New York City. Girls "who had done the unthinkable, unmarried girls who had done what must never be done and given birth" leave their babies in the cradle, ringing the bell nearby, as they disappear into the anonymity of the city.

This scene is described by American writer Anne Roiphe in her poignant book *A Mother's Eye*. As a young girl, Roiphe would peer through the bus window at this small cradle surrounded by ornate stone walls and the gnarled faces of gargoyles. Her mother told her, "the nuns inside the building would wait a discreet amount of time, letting the sinner disappear back into the city streets, and then they would come out and take the baby, foundling that it was, and save its soul and body."

This is the image of adoption 1950s-style. Since then adoption has been maligned as anti-child, anti-woman, anti-black, anti-poor. . . .

Adoption stands like an ignored and forgotten remnant of the past despite a growing band of chronically abused and neglected children who cannot live safely at home with their parents. The causes are many, but domestic violence, substance abuse and mental illness within the family home stand out as the major reasons why parents abuse and neglect their children.

Whatever the reason, when children are removed from the family home, they are subjected to further abuse at the hands of a child welfare system which was built to react to crises rather than provide long-term homes for children. These children endure a disturbingly large number of placements and many never return home. Yet adoption remains unfashionable in child welfare circles. In the year from July 1999 to June

2000, 33,000 children were in out-of-home care across Australia. Only 106 were adopted.

Yet adoption provides many striking examples of children rescued from loveless, deprived childhoods. What has happened to cause such a powerful force for good to become unpopular, even demonised?

## Problems under the Existing System

When the state removes a child from circumstances of chronic abuse or neglect at the hands of parents, providing a safe bed is, understandably, the first priority. But the state's duty of care to these children extends beyond this to a more permanent solution.

Yet as things stand, a child removed from home and made a ward of the state often languishes, until the age of eighteen, in a foster care system based on temporary care. Organisations like Barnardos recount endless examples of this. The case of a boy aged fifteen who has endured twenty-seven placements is not uncommon. Children are bounced back and forth between foster parents and natural parents in the hope that the child's natural parent has overcome a drug habit, recovered from a mental illness, or simply learnt how to care for children.

The unwavering focus on family restoration and parental rights has, for too long, dangerously overshadowed the welfare of the child. It is painfully obvious that biological ties do not guarantee that children will be loved and nurtured. Horrific newspaper stories regularly scream out that young children die in these circumstances.

Unfortunately, the drumbeat of parental rights is louder. The rights of a child to a permanent, loving family is lost in a quagmire of concern for parents and birth families. Too often courts and child welfare professionals are loath to make a judgment as to whether a parent can truly care for a child. . . .

While many children removed from home return successfully to their family, many others cannot. And at some point an effective child welfare system must say that, where parental actions remain dangerously inconsistent with parental good intentions, the child must be removed. The tragic lives of parents are never a reason to repeat the tragedy upon their children. . . .

A child's psychological development hinges upon how they are treated in their early years. Living with chronic abuse or neglect is a recipe for disaster, as is drifting in a system where there is no chance of a child forming attachments. These children learn at an early age that if you form an attachment, it hurts. Many children exhibit atrocious behaviour to ensure they will not be loved. Most remain distant and ultimately become desensitised to life. . . .

## Successful Outcomes of Adoption

The philosophy behind adoption is simple. Childhood is precious and finite. Children should not be forced to do little more than survive for years in a system based on temporary foster care as their parents are given chance after chance to rehabilitate their substance abuse or reform their behaviour. For a one-year-old child, waiting a year for this to happen is a lifetime.

Three years ago Patricia Morgan, research fellow at the Institute of Economic Affairs, launched an attack on what she saw as an ideological opposition in Britain to the adoption of abused and neglected children who had been removed from birth parents. Her book, *Adoption and the Care of Children—The British and American Experience*, was largely responsible for creating a momentum for reform in the UK after she revealed the horrors faced by children who languished for years in temporary foster care while adoption remained unfashionable. Morgan reviewed extensive longitudinal studies and other research and found, to the chagrin of adoption opponents, that outcomes for adopted children are good.

When judging the "success" of adoption, adopted children should be compared with children in circumstances they would have found themselves in had they not been adopted. This means comparing adopted children with foster children, children in institutional care and children restored to birth parents.

The research shows that baby adoptions are the most successful. Breakdown rates are low (under five per cent). The Search Institute of Minneapolis investigated outcomes for the largest ever sample of adoptees in adolescence—a total of 881 children aged between twelve and eighteen who were adopted as babies between 1974 and 1980. As adolescents, over half of these children were found to have high levels of attachment and communication with both parents.

Significantly, when compared to a national sample of adolescents, these adopted adolescents also did well. For example, 54 per cent of adopted adolescents reported high self-esteem compared to 45 per cent of the national sample. Fewer adopted adolescents encountered parental divorce (11 per cent as compared to 28 per cent of the national sample) and fewer lived with sole parents (8 per cent compared to 19 per cent).

The study, says Morgan, found:

Far higher levels of parent-child communication and parental involvement in schooling for adopted adolescents, compared to the national sample. Indeed for positive parent-child relationships, warmth, discipline, positive communication and parents as a social resource, the adopted sample exceeded the levels shown generally and more or less matched the levels for non-adopted siblings. In terms of factors important for children's well-being, adoptive families seem to accentuate the positive and minimize the negative factors.

## A Fifteen-Year-Old Writes about Being Adopted

I was adopted when i was 7 days old, so i haven't ever known anything different . . . i love my adoptive parents very much . . . and i am so happy God put me in this family . . . all my friends know and they dont treat me any different than any body else and that is just how i want it . . . but i would love to one day meet my birth mother . . . but i am happy where i am and if i never get to meet her i know that she loves me or she wouldnt have given me up for adoption so that i could live a better life . . . i get to live out my dreams here . . . i get to ride and show horses . . . and play the sports that i love . . . my adoptive parents are always there for me and are always behind me 100% so if you are adopted and for some reason feel left out or you just dont like the idea . . . look on the bright side you were wanted . . . and you are loved very much . . . and i would encourage you to talk to your adoptive parents about any problem you have with it so that they can help you!

*"I'm Adopted!" Adoption Clubhouse, July 2006,*
*www.adoptionclubhouse.org.*

Morgan also found that outcomes for children adopted late—after the age five—are good:

A study which compared children who had been adopted from care with those who had been returned from care to their parents found that the "restored" children did badly in every respect compared with the adopted children. Very few of the adoptions broke down but a high number of the "restorations" did. Although late-adopted children experience more problems than baby-adoptions, these problems probably have more to do with difficult early experiences prior to adoption than to the adopted status itself.

The research led Morgan to conclude that "adopted children do well because the [adoptive] parents are so keen to rear a child". . . .

## Relinquishing Mothers

Relinquishing mothers tell shocking stories of babies being snatched away from young single mothers in the 1940s before they could set eyes upon their newborn child. Yet many questions have never been publicly aired: What would have happened to those children of unwed teenage mothers if they hadn't been adopted? Was their happiness and well-being so obviously guaranteed without adoption? From the child's perspective, does adoption deserve its sinister reputation? . . .

In Australia, as in the USA and the UK, a small but vociferous group of such women has enjoyed enormous influence over social welfare policy. Cloaked in a mantle of collective guilt, their feminist sisters, child welfare workers and politicians treat adoption like all things of the 1950s era—unjust.

For relinquishing mothers, and their supporters, adoption is an evil means of dealing with the children of unwed mothers. These fanatical opponents to adoption have become worshippers of the womb claiming that children are always better off with birth parents: biology is always the safest bet.

The dark tale they tell of children of adoption suffering inner turmoil, never quite feeling as if they belong in their adoptive family, is unconvincing when exposed to the bright light of reality. The research simply does not support their emotive claims. And we all know adopted children who are happy and indistinguishable, barring biology, from children living with birth parents.

And while some adopted children need to establish biological roots and search for their birth mother, many don't. The story of the tormented adopted child, like that of the relinquishing mother, is of the noisy, well-publicised few. . . .

## Adoption Reform

Internationally, adoption is back on the child welfare agenda. In 1996 President Clinton issued an Executive Memorandum seeking advice on how to increase adoptions not as a means of snatching children from unwed or teenage mothers, but as a means of providing a family to chronically abused and neglected children who have no permanent home.

Since then radical reforms such as adoption quotas and time limits for parents ensure that adoption is a genuine possibility for many of these children. States must file for the termination of parental rights if a child has been in foster care for fifteen of the most recent twenty-two months. The results from such measures are encouraging. In the USA last year 46,000 foster care children were adopted—an increase of 65 per cent on the figure in 1996.

In February 2000, Prime Minister Tony Blair committed the Labour government to a review of adoption and in December of that year, the UK White Paper *Adoption—A New Approach* proposed reforms to ensure that abused and neglected children are given a permanent home.

Adoption is not a happy-ever-after ending for all children. Adolescence is a melting pot of emotions for most children, adopted or not, as they search for their place in the world. Some adopted children may experience a period of upheaval, but one can only wonder at what these children might have experienced had they not been adopted into a family.

Breakdown rates for adoption are about 9 per cent. However, the younger the child is at placement, the more likely the adoption will succeed. And tragically, hundreds of children across Australia remain in temporary care for years while adoption is portrayed as sinister. If adoption continues as an option of last resort, children will remain in the limbo of foster care for too long. Adoption needs to be embraced, not as a punishment for unfit parents, but as a gift of loving for the child.

To date [in 2002], adoption has been sadly maligned in Australia by a vocal band of relinquishing mothers, feminists, indigenous leaders and child welfare workers. However, moves in New South Wales indicate that attitudes are changing. The challenge for all those involved in the child welfare system is to ensure that any change in government policy is based on knowledge, rather than ideology.

| *"There are worries about miscarriage, chromosomal disorders like Down's, high blood pressure, and diabetes."*

# Older Mothers Face Health Risks

*Maxine Frith*

*Maxine Frith is the social affairs correspondent for* The Independent *newspaper in London. The percentage of first-time mothers older than the age of thirty-five tripled between 1990 and 2002, in part because of innovations and advancements in infertility treatment. The following viewpoint details the myriad of significant health risks that face any woman who gets pregnant after the age of forty, even if she has been pregnant before.*

As you read, consider the following questions:

1. What dangers can result from hypertension during pregnancy?

2. Why do doctors recommend using eggs donated by family members during fertility treatment?

3. What genetic trait might contribute to the advanced-age fertility in a group of Ashkenazi Jewish women?

Maxine Frith, "Women in Their 40s Put Health at Risk by Getting Pregnant," *The Independent (Online Edition)*, June 22, 2005. Copyright © 2005 Independent News and Media Limited. Reproduced by permission.

Women who delay motherhood until their forties are at greatly increased risk of suffering difficult pregnancies, miscarriage or dying during childbirth, a leading obstetrician has said.

Doctors are failing to tell women about the risks involved in having children later in life, according to Professor Michael de Swiet, an obstetric physician at Queen Charlotte's Hospital in London. He said doctors should "stop playing God" by allowing women in their mid-forties and over to have fertility treatment, and called for more debate on the personal and social implications of older parents.

The number of women having their first child when they are 35 or over has more than tripled in the past 15 years. In 1990, just 3 per cent of first-time mothers were over 35, but by 2002, the proportion had risen to 10 per cent. For women over 42 more than half of all pregnancies end in miscarriage or stillbirth.

## Late Pregnancy and Health Complications

Professor De Swiet said that for women aged 20 to 24 in Britain, the risk of dying during childbirth was just 7.3 per 100,000. But for women over 40, the rate rose to 35.5—a level comparable to countries such as Armenia and Iran.

Women who conceive in their forties are also at increased risk of hypertension—high blood pressure which can lead to pre-eclampsia, a condition which can be fatal for both mother and unborn child.

The risks even affect women who start having children in their early thirties, when there is less risk, but go on getting pregnant as they reach their forties.

A woman over 35 who already has at least two children and then becomes pregnant again is 100 times more likely to die from a blood clot than a first-time 20-year-old mother.

Professor De Swiet, who specialises in treating complications during pregnancy, said: "I have had 90 women in my

**Older Fathers Increase Risk of Down Syndrome with Older Mothers**

Rate of Down syndrome per 100,000 births by maternal and paternal age in New York State, 1983 to 1997

| Paternal Age | No./100,000 Births | | | | |
| --- | --- | --- | --- | --- | --- |
| | Maternal Age 24 or Younger | Maternal Age 25–29 | Maternal Age 30–34 | Maternal Age 35–39 | Maternal Age 40 or Older |
| 24 or Younger | 64 | 80 | 87 | 131 | 314 |
| 25–29 | 59 | 72 | 100 | 158 | 395 |
| 30–34 | 57 | 58 | 105 | 174 | 578 |
| 35–39 | 90 | 78 | 104 | 189 | 427 |
| 40 or Older | 48 | 66 | 99 | 222 | 632 |

TAKEN FROM: Harry Fisch et al., "The Influence of Paternal Age on Down Syndrome," *The Journal of Urology*, volume 169 (June 2003), pp. 2275.

clinic in the last year over the age of 40 and I do have concerns. There are worries about miscarriage, chromosomal disorders like Down's, high blood pressure and diabetes.

## Doctors and Patients Ignore Risks

"At the moment, doctors are not telling women about the risks, and even when they do, the women often don't take it in. What you have to remember is that some of these women who become pregnant with IVF techniques are fundamentally unwell—they are not good breeders and they are at high risk of both morbidity and mortality."

It was not simply life-threatening conditions that affected older expectant mothers, Professor De Swiet said. "They seem to be more at risk from what I call the misery factor during pregnancy," he explained. "They tend to suffer more from breathlessness, heart palpitations and fainting. Often by 35 weeks, they have had enough and come in demanding a Caesarean."

He said that women should ideally have their children between 25 and 35, be aware that between 35 and 45 they were "safe enough" but that over that age, they should be made fully aware of the dangers.

He added: "I don't think it is for us as doctors to play God. Society must discuss as to how we should judge who should have pregnancy at an extreme age."

## Donated Eggs and Egg Quality

In a separate study, scientists found that women who use donated eggs from non-family members to become pregnant are at increased risk of miscarriage and pre-eclampsia. They suggested that, where possible, women who cannot use their own eggs should ask their sisters to donate in order to reduce the risks to their health and to their unborn child.

Older women in particular often need to use donated eggs because their own are not good enough for IVF procedures.

Researchers in Korea studied 61 women who became pregnant using donated eggs and compared them with expectant mothers who underwent IVF treatment using their own eggs.

The scientists believe eggs from an unrelated donor may lead to the introduction of "foreign elements" to the developing placenta and trigger abnormal responses.

## Is Late Fertility an Inherited Trait?

When Cherie Blair gave birth to her fourth child at the age of 45, the Prime Minister was widely admired for his virility and uniqueness at becoming a father while in office.

But it may be that the conception of Leo, now five, was down to Mrs Blair's genes rather than her husband's potency. Scientists have identified a certain type of genetic make-up in women who have continued to be able to become pregnant naturally over the age of 45.

Researchers from the Hadassah University Hospital in Jerusalem studied 250 Ashkenazi Jewish women, all of whom had children in their late forties and all of whom did not use contraception. Eighty per cent of the women in the study had at least six children, as well as a low miscarriage rate.

The researchers tested eight of the women and studied their genetic make-up compared to a control group of non-Ashkenazi women. They found the Ashkenazi women had a pattern of gene expression which appeared to protect against DNA damage and cell death in the ovaries.

Dr Neri Laufer, who led the research, said his team had proved that the "pregnancy" genes were not unique to these particular Jewish women because they had also been found in Bedouin women.

He added: "We hope that this will lead to better understanding of the ageing process and improve our ability to preserve fertility in older women."

*"We shouldn't jump to the conclusion that it's wrong for women to become mothers at this age."*

# Older Mothers Do Not Face Health Risks

*Mark Henderson*

*Mark Henderson is a science editor at the* Times *newspaper in London. He attended the conference of the American Society for Reproductive Medicine in New Orleans in 2006. In the following viewpoint, he reports on findings that women older than fifty years of age who conceive and bear children via in vitro fertilization are at no more physical or psychological risk during pregnancy and motherhood than younger women undergoing the same treatment. The scientists who performed the research argue that maternal age should not be a consideration when doctors choose candidates for artificial reproduction treatments.*

As you read, consider the following questions:

1. Why are women older than fifty considered poor candidates for in vitro fertilization?

2. What methods did scientists use to determine the effects of pregnancy and motherhood on older women?

Mark Henderson, "Becoming a Mother at 50 'No Risk to Health'," *TimesOnline*, October 23, 2006. Copyright © 2006 Times Newspapers Ltd. Reproduced by permission.

3. What concerns about women who become pregnant late in life (and their children) do critics have?

The first study to investigate the parenting experiences of older IVF [the acronym for in vitro fertilization, an artificial reproduction technology in which eggs are fertilized outside a woman's body and then implanted into her uterus] mothers has revealed that they cope equally well with the stress of motherhood as those who have children in their thirties and forties, and are no more likely to suffer physical or psychological ill health.

The findings come only a week after Lord Harries of Pentregarth, who chairs the Government's fertility watchdog, argued that maternal age should not be a sufficient reason to refuse IVF treatment, and provide the best evidence yet in support of his case.

## Doctors, not Government, Should Judge IVF Candidates

In an interview with the *Times* last weekend, the former Bishop of Oxford rejected calls for a strict upper-age limit, saying that he respected the decisions of women such as Patricia Rashbrook, who had a son at the age of 62 this year after travelling abroad for therapy. Doctors should instead be left to choose patients according to their own clinical judgment.

While there is no absolute age limit for IVF in Britain, the NHS [National Health Service] will not fund it for women aged over 40, and it is difficult in practice for those aged over 45 to find even private clinics that are willing to treat them. Though use of eggs from young donors can cut the risk of genetic defects, which is higher for older natural mothers, low success rates and laws requiring doctors to consider the welfare of IVF children still lead most fertility units to reject older women as patients. Only 24 women over 50 had IVF births in 2002, the last year for which figures are available [as of 2006].

## Aleta St. James, 57, speaks about Becoming a Mother Late in Life

I got to a point at about forty-nine.... I've had a very extensive career, traveled all over, I found myself, I'm at a point now where I really want to look at what my personal goals are.... And I realized that what it was was children....

I went through a series of, um, trying to do it naturally and didn't work—three miscarriages—and I realized that if I really wanted to go for it, to really have children and carry them naturally, I was gonna have to go the in vitro route....

By the time I was fifty-seven, I was having twins! ...

To me fifty is the new thirty....

I have a friend who is a kung fu master, he says to me, "Aleta, I will be better when I am eighty than when I'm sixty." That's what I'm connecting to. Chita Rivera, do you remember her? She was in *West Side Story?*...

She's seventy-three. Now she's dancing up a storm on Broadway. Better than ever at seventy-three.... When my children are twenty I'm going to be kicking up a storm unless God just decides otherwise and takes me out....

You know, it's all your mindset and how you live your life. My children, I hope I will give them a strong enough foundation and a support group of loving family and friends ... It's not just about me staying around, it's the quality of life I've given them, how much I've loved them.

*Will Femia, "Audio Chat: Aleta St. James, New Mom at 57,"*
*December 19, 2005, www.msnbc.com.*

Numbers are also kept low because these patients generally need donated eggs to conceive, but the number of older mothers is expected to grow significantly in the future. New technology now allows women in their twenties or thirties to preserve their fertility by freezing eggs, which could be implanted in their fifties with a good chance of success.

## Risks Associated with Pregnancy after Age Fifty

Controversy surrounding the issue of older mothers centres on the likely impact on their physical and mental health, and that of their children.

Older women, particularly those over 55, have a higher risk of pregnancy complications such as pre-eclampsia, and many people question their capacity to care for their children as they grow old themselves. Dr Rashbrook, for example, will be 80 when her son turns 18.

The new research from the University of Southern California (USC) indicates that at least some of these concerns are misplaced. "There is reason to say, in the absence of other data, that maybe we shouldn't jump to the conclusion that it's wrong for women to become mothers at this age," said Anne Steiner, who conducted the work with Richard Paulson.

In the study, which will be presented tomorrow [October 24, 2006] at the American Society for Reproductive Medicine conference in New Orleans, the researchers investigated 49 women who had given birth at 50 or over between 1992 and 2004, after treatment with donated eggs at the USC clinic.

Each was matched with an IVF mother in her thirties and another in her forties, and all were sent questionnaires about physical and mental functioning and parenting stress.

The results showed no significant differences between the three groups on any of these measures. If anything, the oldest mothers suffered slightly fewer psychological problems than younger ones.

## Analyzing the Research

Dr Steiner, who has since moved to the University of North Carolina, cautioned that as the oldest children in the study were 13 when it began it was not possible to draw conclusions about parenting of teenagers. Even so, she said it supports Lord Harries's view.

"The conclusion from this study, though it is limited and of a small size, is that, if we look from the perspective of stress and physical and mental functioning, it doesn't seem like we can restrict parenting based on these reasons." She also pointed out that older women in the study tended to have younger partners, and that this may influence their ability to cope.

Dr Paulson said opposition to older mothers rests not on evidence that they make poor parents, but on prejudice.

"Society still has these feelings about motherhood. The way we view the mother is much more circumscribed than for the father: she should be young and attractive. That is underneath all this talk about the ethics and legality of treating older women. Deep down, society has a fixed idea of what motherhood should be, and this causes deep discomfort."

Bill Ledger, of the University of Sheffield, said that while the research was welcome it did not address all his reservations about giving IVF to women in their fifties. "It does not surprise me that they cope well with young children while they're in their fifties, but what no one has looked at yet is what happens when these children are 18. It worries me that their parents will be in their seventies and eighties. I have yet to be convinced that a child will have a good quality of life if its parents are older than its friends' grandparents."

# Periodical Bibliography

*The following articles have been selected to supplement the diverse views presented in this chapter.*

Peggy Butler — "Secret Confessions of a Childless Black Woman: Where Is It Written that All Women Were Meant to Have Children?" *off our backs*, April 2006.

*Economist* — "Making Babies, the Hard Way," May 19, 2007.

Leah Eckberg Feldman — "The Sisters They Never Knew," *Good Housekeeping*, May 2006.

Kate Johnson — "Strict IVF Regulations Could Lower Success Rates," *Family Practice News*, December 15, 2006.

Mary Ann Moon — "Older Paternal Age Tied to Autism in Offspring," *Clinical Psychiatry News*, October 2006.

Liza Mundy — "Souls on Ice: America's Human Embryo Glut and the Unbearable Lightness of Almost Being," *Mother Jones*, July–August 2006.

Patty Onderko — "Younger vs. Older Moms (Survey)," *Baby Talk*, September 2006.

Anne-Marie O'Neill — "Why Are American Babies Being Adopted Abroad? A Little-Known Trend—European and Canadian Families Adopting Black Infants from the U.S.—Stirs an Emotional Debate," *People Weekly*, June 6, 2005.

Ann Powers — "Sharing Rebecca," *Parenting*, December 2006.

Carol Sanger — "Infant Safe Haven Laws: Legislating the Culture of Life," *Conscience*, Spring 2007.

Susan Schindehette — "Comeback Kid: Abandoned Baby Ashley Wyrick," *People Weekly*, July 17, 2006.

OPPOSING
VIEWPOINTS®
SERIES

# CHAPTER 3

# How Does Divorce Affect Children?

# Chapter Preface

Tales of romantic love are as numerous as those of legally sanctioned divorce. It seems that in the early 2000s passion brings people together and drives them apart at ever-increasing rates. A publication put out by the National Marriage Project, "The State of Our Unions, 2001: The Social Health of Marriage in America," estimated that around 42 percent of all marriages end in divorce, a rate that is about twice as high as the rate in 1960.

Americans who speak for "traditional, conservative values" blame the 1960s counterculture practices of free love and self-indulgence for introducing what they perceive as the lack of commitment to marriage. To a great extent, this social revolution inspired people to look beyond what was expected of them and to pursue personal fulfillment. But it's plausible that the idealization of the traditional, conservative view of marriage has overtaken the reality of it. Television shows of the 1950s and 1960s portrayed marriage as a stable state with only minor conflict, in which mothers and fathers were content to play their roles. Even the somewhat revolutionary *Brady Bunch*, which portrayed a large stepfamily, emphasized the happiness husbands and wives could find in each other's company and promoted the idea that spouses in a second marriage could rely on each other to solve all their problems.

By contrast to television characters, real-life couples who get married discover early that their relationships are not perfect. The disconnection between expectations and reality is likely the source of much tension and conflict within a marriage. Previous generations viewed marriage as a means for begetting children and providing security and a home; love often played a role in choosing a partner, but it was not the impetus behind making the commitment. Once the ideals and expectations of romantic love were juxtaposed with the challenge of finding a compatible economic partner and partner in childrearing, marriage became much harder to perfect.

The feminist movement of the 1960s and 1970s encouraged women to develop an identity outside the home and not to let their desires be subsumed by the responsibilities of raising a family and keeping house. Stanford sociology professor Paula England and her research colleagues, sociologists David Cotter and Joan Hermsen, reported in 2006 that 65 percent of mothers with children in preschool worked at least part-time, compared to only 30 percent who did so in 1970; the number of working mothers of school-age children increased from 56 to 79 percent during the same time period. As women make their own additions to the family coffers, the relationships between husbands and wives change. Men expect financial assistance from their wives; women expect household assistance from their husbands. Marriage in the twenty-first century in the United States resembles more an equal partnership than the division of labor exhibited between the husband/breadwinner and wife/homemaker in earlier decades.

In the early 2000s, men and women are considered marital partners instead of complementary figures, and the pressure to find the perfect partner is even stronger. Women earn their own money and no longer feel so dependent on men. Single adults seek their "soul mates" and marriage. But do high divorce rates signify a lack of faith in marriage? According to a 2002 report by the National Center for Health Statistics, 75 percent of divorced women remarried within ten years; according to a 2000 paper by Wendy Manning, Susan Stewart, and Pamela Smock at the Center for Family and Demographic Research, 75 percent of divorced men remarried within five years. The impetus to find a better partner and try marriage again implies that there is no decline of interest in being married.

Were the world made of only adults, it is doubtful that the rates of divorce and remarriage would draw much attention.

Children, however, are often in the middle of divorce, generating fights over custody, child support, and parenting techniques. Is the adult quest for a completely personally fulfilling marriage destroying the family it intends to improve? The authors in the following chapter discuss the effects of divorce and remarriage on the children caught in the middle, both in the immediate and long-term future.

| "Any and all sorts of abuse and exploitation would be seen to occur at higher rates in steprelationships than in genetic parent-child relationships."

# Stepchildren Face Extra Risk of Abuse

## Martin Daly and Margo Wilson

*Martin Daly is a professor of psychology at McMaster University in Hamilton, Ontario, Canada. He specializes in the relevance of evolution and ecology to human psychology. Margo Wilson, also a professor of psychology at McMaster University, is interested in interpersonal conflict and violence. The two authors frequently collaborate. The following viewpoint presents evidence to support the existence of the phenomenon known as the "Cinderella effect." Taken from the Cinderella fairy tale, in which a young girl is abused and neglected by her stepmother and stepsisters, the Cinderella effect describes the high incidence of harm done to children by stepparents.*

As you read, consider the following questions:

1. If the actual numbers of small children killed by a stepparent are smaller than the actual numbers of small

children killed by a genetic parent, why do the authors point to these statistics as evidence of the Cinderella effect?

2. What are some possible arguments for the hypothesis that stepparents in the home may not be the reason that some small children face an increased risk of death or harm?

3. What are some examples of non-violent discrimination against stepchildren?

Parents commit a huge amount of time, attention and material resources to the care of their children, as well as incurring life-threatening risks to defend them and bodily depletion to nourish them. Why are parents motivated to invest so heavily in their children? From an evolutionary perspective, the answer is surely that natural selection has favoured intensive parental care in our lineage. Those ancestral genotypes and phenotypes that best succeeded in raising children to become reproducing adults were the ones that persisted and proliferated. . . .

Stepparental care, unlike modern adoption, is cross-culturally ubiquitous and almost certainly ancient. It is also not peculiar to human beings, and its distribution in the animal kingdom lends support to the idea that the reason why such care occurs is because investing resources in a new mate's young of prior unions is a part of "mating effort", confined to species in which suitable mates are scarce and in which couples, once established, often stay together for longer than just one breeding season. . . . However, a stepchild must rarely have been as valuable to a stepparent's expected fitness as a child of one's own would be, and we may therefore anticipate that stepparents will not, in general, feel such whole-hearted, self-sacrificial love for their wards as genetic parents so often do.

It is on these grounds that we hypothesized, many years ago, that any and all sorts of abuse and exploitation would be seen to occur at higher rates in steprelationships than in genetic parent-child relationships. . . . This hypothesis has since been abundantly supported in our own research and in that of many others. This differential (mis)treatment is what we refer to as the "Cinderella effect."

## Fatal Batterings of Small Children

This most severe category of child maltreatment exhibits Cinderella effects of the greatest magnitude: in several countries, stepparents beat very young children to death at per capita rates that are *more than 100 times higher* than the corresponding rates for genetic parents.

The most thorough analyses are for Canada, where data in a national archive of all homicides known to police indicate that children under 5 years of age were beaten to death by their putative genetic fathers at a rate of 2.6 deaths per million child-years at risk (residing with their fathers) in 1974–1990, while the corresponding rate for stepfathers was over 120 times greater at 321.6 deaths per million child-years at risk. Note that because few small children *have* stepfathers, this rate differential does not, in itself, convey anything about the absolute numbers of victims; what these rates represent are 74 fatal batterings by genetic fathers in 28.3 million child-years at risk, and 55 by stepfathers in 0.17 million child-years at risk. . . .

According to an analysis of the FBI's *Supplementary Homicide Reports* (SHR) case data, stepfathers [in the United States] beat children under 5 years old to death at a rate of 55.9 per million children at risk per annum, compared to 5.6 for genetic fathers. This 10-fold risk differential, albeit substantial, is surprisingly low in comparison to what has been documented in Canada, Britain and Australia, but there is good reason to believe that it is an extreme underestimate. The main reason for saying this is that SHR coders are instructed to restrict the "stepparent" code to persons in registered marriages and to code "mothers' boyfriends", whether they coreside or not, as nonrelatives. In contrast, genetic fathers are coded as "fathers" regardless of marital status, and so [the] comparison is effectively one of married stepfathers *versus* married *and* unmarried genetic fathers.

Swedish data indicate a smaller, but still substantial, Cinderella effect with respect to parental homicides *in toto*, (i.e. not just fatal batterings). . . . Toddlers were found to have been killed by genetic parents at a rate of 3.8 per million coresiding parent-child dyads [pairs] per annum, while the corresponding rate for stepparents was 8.4 times greater at 31.7 deaths per million dyads per annum. . . .

## Nonlethal Abuse

The evidence for Cinderella effects in nonlethal abuse is much more extensive than that for homicides. Numerous studies from a diversity of countries indicate that stepparents perpetrate both nonlethal physical assaults and sexual abuse at much higher rates than genetic parents.

One sort of evidence comes from the case data collected by child protection agencies, in which stepfamily households and stepparent perpetrators are greatly overrepresented relative to their prevalence in the population-at-large. . . . Another source of evidence is victimization surveys, from which comparisons can be made between the responses of those who live or formerly lived with stepparents and those raised by genetic parents. The former routinely report much higher rates of both physical and sexual abuse. . . .

When runaway and homeless adolescents are interviewed, a very large proportion report that they have fled stepfamilies in which they were subject to abuse.

## Portrayal of a Stepmother from Another Time and Culture

### The Story of Yeh-Shen (9th-Century China)

During the time of the Ch'in and Han dynasties, a cave chief named Wu married two wives and each gave birth to baby girls. Before long Chief Wu and one wife died leaving one baby, Yeh-Shen, to be reared by her stepmother. The stepmother didn't like Yeh-Shen for she was more beautiful and kinder than her own daughter so she treated her poorly. Yeh-Shen was given the worse jobs and the only friend she had was a beautiful fish with big golden eyes. Each day the fish came out of the water onto the bank to be fed by Yeh-Shen. Now Yeh-Shen had little food for herself but she was willing to share with the fish. Her stepmother hearing about the fish, disguised herself as Yeh-Shen and enticed the fish from the water. She stabbed it with a dagger, and cooked the fish for dinner.

*Ai-Ling Louie,* Yeh-Shen,
*New York: Philomel Books, 1982.*

## What Causes the Cinderella Effect?

That stepparents abuse and kill children at much higher *per capita* rates than genetic parents does not necessarily implicate the steprelationship as a causal factor. It could instead be correlated ("confounded", in statistical jargon) with some other factor that is of more direct relevance.

An obvious example of a possible confound is socioeconomic status: one might hypothesize that the stresses of poverty cause the poor to be especially likely to abuse and kill their children and also to experience high rates of divorce and remarriage, making steprelationship an incidental correlate of abuse. This initially plausible hypothesis has been tested and rejected with respect to Cinderella effects in Canada and the U.S. In both countries, poverty is indeed a risk factor for child maltreatment, but ... having a stepparent and being poor are in large measure independent and additive ("orthogonal") predictors of the risk that a child will be abused.

A final confound hypothesis is that there are "personality" differences between parents who reside with only their own children and people who become stepparents. . . .

Although the population of persons who become stepparents may indeed be atypical of parents in general, one line of evidence speaks against the idea that this could account for Cinderella effects: abusive stepparents typically spare their own children. In a study of abusive families in the U.S., for example, only the stepchildren were abused in every one of 10 households containing both stepchildren and children of the current marital union; similarly, in urban Canadian samples, the stepchildren were selectively abused in 9 of 10 such families in one study and in 19 of 22 in another . . .

## Stepfathers or "Mothers' Boyfriends"?

In our own research and in the review above, we typically define a "stepparent" as the coresiding partner of a (presumed) genetic parent, regardless of marital registration. But marital status may not be irrelevant, and a large proportion of slain and abused stepchildren were the victims of their mothers' "live-in boyfriends". This raises the question of whether Cinderella effects might be due primarily, or even solely, to abuse by *de facto* stepparents rather than registered-marriage stepparents. The answer is that Cinderella effects are large regardless of marital registration. Both registered-marriage stepfathers and *de facto* stepfathers (*aka* commonlaw stepfathers, mothers' boyfriends, cohabitees, and, in older literature, "paramours") are overrepresented as perpetrators of abuse in many of the studies cited above. . . .

The most thorough examination of the simultaneous relevance of steprelationship and marital registration is that conducted by [M.] Daly & [M.] Wilson (2001) with respect to fatal batterings in Canada. What they found was that both steprelationship and commonlaw status were strong predictors of homicide risk, and that neither variable's influence could be explained away as an artifact of the other's. In other words, stepfathers were greatly overrepresented as killers within both registered and *de facto* unions considered separately, and *de facto* fathers were greatly overrepresented within both genetic and stepfathers considered separately.

## Stepparents or Stepfathers?

Many of the analyses discussed above have focused on homicides and abuse perpetrated by stepfathers *vs.* (putative) genetic fathers. Can we infer that excess risk is a feature only of stepfather homes and not stepmother homes? The answer is no. The reason why stepmothers are often omitted from the data presentation is because small children live with stepmothers so infrequently that in all but the largest databases, the cases are usually so few that estimates of abuse risk are unreliable, changing markedly as a result of the addition or subtraction of a single case. Nevertheless, all available evidence indicates that excess risk from stepmothers (relative to genetic mothers) is roughly on the same order as excess risk from stepfathers (relative to genetic fathers).

The best evidence on this question comes from large child abuse databases. . . . Studies included large numbers of stepmother cases and provided evidence that rates of physical abuse in stepmother and stepfather households are roughly similar and far in excess of those in two-genetic-parent households. Stepmothers are also substantially and significantly more likely to kill young children than genetic mothers according to analyses of U.S. data, despite the facts that (1) as with stepfathers, the code "stepmother" was restricted to those in registered marriages, and (2) the genetic mother cases included neonaticides, a distinct category of homicides that is sometimes quite numerous. Finally, stepmother households tend to be even more extremely overrepresented than stepfather households among adolescent runaways who aver that they are fleeing abusive families.

## Non-Abusive Discrimination against Stepchildren

It is important to stress that although stepchildren incur elevated risks of abuse and homicide, these dire outcomes are by no means typical. Many, perhaps most, stepparents make positive contributions to the well-being of their stepchildren, and most stepparents and stepchildren evaluate their relationships at least somewhat positively. Nevertheless, steprelationships are difficult, and those who make it their business to help stepfamilies in distress are unanimous in cautioning that it is a mistake to expect that a stepparent-stepchild relationship is, or will with time become, psychologically equivalent to a birthparent-child relationship. Research tells the same story.... [In] a select sample of well-established, "successful", middle class, registered-marriage U.S. stepfamilies, ... only 53% of the stepfathers and 25% of the stepmothers felt able to say that they had any "parental feeling" (much less "love") for their stepchildren. There are literally hundreds of self-help manuals for stepfamily members, and they have a single focus: how to cope with the characteristic conflicts of stepfamily life.

In light of the theoretical ideas that we espoused at the beginning of this review and facts like those recounted above, we long ago proposed that violence against stepchildren would prove to be the atypical and extreme "tip of the iceberg" of a more ubiquitous discrimination. A wide variety of recent research in diverse disciplines has now demonstrated that this is indeed the case.

Econometric analyses of large databases such as the U.S. *Panel Study of Income Dynamics* provide one sort of evidence: controlling for the family's economic means, U.S. stepchildren receive reduced investment in the form of support for higher education, routine medical and dental care, and even food. Surveys that ask people directly about parental support tell the same story: according to both the parents and the children, stepparents withhold investment relative to genetic parents. Also of interest in this context is [the] finding that both the mothers and stepfathers in British stepfamily homes expressed low aspirations for the children's education, lower even than those of single mothers of lesser means.

Another sort of evidence comes from anthropological studies using observational sampling methods. In one such study of Trinidadian villagers, . . . stepfathers spent significantly less time with their children than genetic fathers, and that a significantly higher proportion of their interactions were "agonistic". In another such study of Hadza hunter-gatherers in Tanzania, . . . although stepfathers mind their stepchildren in camp, they are unlike genetic fathers in their behaviour towards them; for example, they never play with them. Stepchildren also suffer elevated rates of accidental injury, both lethal and nonlethal, from infancy onwards, apparently because they are less assiduously monitored and protected and they suffer elevated mortality in general, not just from assaults.

In view of all the above, it is no surprise to learn that stepchildren find their home life stressful. Many studies have reported that they leave home at a substantially younger age than children from intact birth families and not only do they leave earlier, but they are far more likely to cite family conflict as the reason. The last findings that we will cite are from a study of child health in Dominica: stepchildren exhibit reduced growth and have chronically higher circulating levels of the stress hormone cortisol than their age mates living with only their genetic parents under similar material circumstances in the same village.

Let us stress again that most stepparents try hard to treat their stepchildren fairly, and extreme negative outcomes, despite being much more prevalent than in genetic-parent homes, are infrequent. That said, however, it is also important to recognize that Cinderella is no fairy tale.

*"Humans may be genetically pro-*
*grammed to prefer their genetic off-*
*spring over other children. But factors*
*other than biology also matter in shap-*
*ing parenting desires and capacities."*

# Stepchildren Do Not
# Face Extra Risk of Abuse

*Elizabeth Bartholet*

*Elizabeth Bartholet is professor of law and faculty director of the*
*Child Advocacy Program at Harvard Law School, where she*
*teaches civil rights and family law, specializing in child welfare,*
*adoption, and reproductive technology. In the following view-*
*point, the author argues that sociobiology and evolutionary*
*theory provide no compelling evidence that children face in-*
*creased danger from stepparents than they do from biological*
*parents. Although humans may be genetically programmed to*
*prefer their own children, they are not animals; they have the*
*ability to love outside blood relationships both for their own*
*sakes and for the benefit of society.*

Elizabeth Bartholet, "Guiding Principles for Picking Parents," *Harvard Journal of Law & Gender*, vol. 27, 2004. Copyright © 2006 by the President and Fellows of Harvard College. Reproduced by permission.

As you read, consider the following questions:

1. Why is it time for society to reconsider how a person's parentage is defined?

2. Beyond the fact that a stepparent exists, what are some unique characteristics of a stepparent family that may explain higher incidences of abuse and neglect of stepchildren?

3. What are some examples of successful relationships between adults and children who are not genetically related to them?

DNA tests can determine whether there is a genetic link between two people—whether a given man's sperm helped create a given child—but not whether that man is or is not that child's *parent*. In fact, biology has never been all-determinative in defining parentage, whether in nature or under law. In nature some animals are raised by both biological parents, but in most species "fathers" exist only in the sense that they create life. Further, like humans, animals sometimes "adopt" others' offspring. . . .

Many of our societal rules for defining parentage were developed in an era when children were ordinarily the genetic product of the husband and wife who raised them, and it was in any event difficult to know if they were not. The world has changed. We now have DNA tests that can easily and conclusively establish whether or not there is any genetic link between parent and child. We now have a significant breakdown in the nuclear family, with men and women moving with far greater freedom in and out of different marital and marital-like relationships, same-sex as well as opposite-sex, and with children more often being raised at least in part by stepparents or stepparent equivalents. We now have reproductive technologies that enable the use of third parties' eggs, sperm, gestational services, and embryos to produce children to be raised by parents who may have no genetic or biological con-

## Age and Stepparent/ Stepchild Bonding

**Young children under the age of 10** may find the adjustment easier because they thrive on close, cohesive family relationships. The forces that draw a stepfamily together coincide with the need of young children for emotional involvement and structure. Youngsters are usually more accepting of a new adult in the family, especially when the adult is a positive influence. These children, however, are quick to feel a sense of abandonment or competition if they think their parent is devoting more time and energy to the new spouse than to them.

**Adolescents aged 10–14** may have the most difficult time adjusting to a stepfamily. They tend to be oppositional. Because of their sensitivity, stepparents need to be especially aware of having time to bond with them before stepping in as a disciplinarian or authority figure.

**Teens aged 15 or older** need less parenting and may have less involvement in stepfamily life. Older adolescents prefer to separate from the family as they form their own identities. They are less interested in closeness and bonding. Furthermore, since they are more sensitive to expressions of affection and sexuality, they may be disturbed by an active romance in their family.

*Jaelline Jaffe, Jeanne Segal, and Sheila Hutman,*
*"Blended Families/Stepfamilies,"*
*Helpguide, 2007, www.helpguide.org.*

nection to them. This newly available DNA information, these newly complex family arrangements, and these new reproductive technologies have together produced a raft of new questions about how to define parentage. . . .

## Genetics and the Law

Parenting law has often defined as parents persons who have no biological link to the child in preference over those who have such a link. Traditionally state law has defined husbands as parents of the children born to their wives during the marriage, regardless of any evidence that might exist indicating that other men were actually the sperm fathers. Adoption law defines as full legal parents persons who have no biological link to the child. For decades state law has defined husbands as the fathers of children their wives produce using sperm from other men through artificial insemination. . . .

Sociobiology, or evolutionary psychology, is enjoying something of a revival today, providing new energy for claims that genetics should play a yet more important role than it has traditionally in defining parentage. Some of its adherents claim that, because of "biological favoritism," child rearing by nonrelatives is "inherently problematic." They say that human beings, like the rest of the animal kingdom, are genetically programmed to produce and to favor their own progeny over others': "It is not that unrelated individuals are unable to do the job of parenting, it is just that they are not as likely to do the job well." Richard Dawkins, who has done much to popularize evolutionary psychology, describes adoption as a "mistake," a "misfiring of a built-in rule." He claims that "the generous female is doing her own genes no good by caring for the orphan. She is wasting time and energy that could be invested in the lives of her own kin, particularly future children of her own." Martin Daly and Margo Wilson, leading proponents of evolutionary psychology, write in their well-known *Homicide* book:

> Perhaps the most obvious prediction from a Darwinian view of parental motives is this: Substitute parents will generally tend to care less profoundly for children than natural parents, with the result that children reared by people other than their natural parents will be more often exploited and

133

otherwise at risk. Parental investment is a precious resource, and selection must favor those parental psyches that do not squander it on nonrelatives.

Sexual strategies theory promotes a related claim—that men are genetically programmed to choose women who will faithfully raise their progeny. Thus, when DNA evidence shows that a child a man thought was his biological child is not his, revealing that the woman has betrayed him, he reacts with anger toward both the woman and the child.

## Critiques of Evolutionary Explanations

Evolutionary theorizing of this kind has been subject to powerful critiques in recent years. While it does seem likely that biology *matters* in parenting, as the sociobiologists quoted above claim, the important issues are how much it matters, how much factors other than biology, including socialization, matter, and what values we want to promote. Evolutionary theory provides little help in addressing these issues.

Sociobiologists who promote the biological favoritism theory have produced little empirical support for its validity in the realm of human parenting. Those claiming that empirical support exists all point to researchers Daly and Wilson's well-known study of stepparenting. This study purports to provide empirical grounding for the biological favoritism claim, by demonstrating higher rates of abuse, both physical and sexual, in stepparent households and by stepparents as compared to genetically related parents within households. However, some highly respected research questions the generally accepted conclusion that stepparents are in fact disproportionately responsible for abuse. Even assuming the higher abuse rates claimed, Daly and Wilson's arguments are notably unpersuasive because they fail entirely to address the many obvious factors other than genetics that could explain disproportionate abuse in stepparent households.

These [factors] include, but are by no means limited to: that a stepparent is by definition not the legal parent, creating obvious issues as to parenting authority; that a legal out-of-household parent will often exist, competing with any parental role played by the stepparent; that stepparents will usually enter the family after the child has established parenting relationships with others; that stepparent households are, as the authors concede, generally more contentious and unhappy; that stepchildren typically bring problems to the family dynamics; and that sexual relationships between stepparents and stepchildren are not subject to the same taboo as those between biologically linked parents and children.

Evolutionary theorists themselves argue that stepparent and particularly stepfather relationships are more problematic than other nongenetic parenting relationships because men are genetically programmed to demand that women devote themselves to nurturing the men's genetic product, and we are all programmed to resist "exploitation of one partner's efforts for the other's fitness benefit." . . .

## Love Really Can Conquer All

The stepparent evidence is in any event countered by powerful evidence that looks in the opposite direction, which these sociobiologists fail to address in any significant way. Adoption studies show adoptive parent-child relationships working essentially as well as biological parent-child relationships. Daly and Wilson admit that adoption apparently does work well, without ever adequately explaining how this could be true if genetics are so central to parenting capacity. . . .

[Researchers June] Carbone and [Naomi] Cahn's analysis of studies of fathers who move from one adult relationship to another show that these men appear to care more for the nonrelated children with whom they are living than the related children they left behind. Apparently, any "biological favoritism" that may exist is outweighed by the adult relation-

135

ship factor. Carbone and Cahn show that biological favoritism theorists typically fail to take into account the complexity of human beings and their institutional lives:

> Humans act not just through direct provisions for their children and indifference (or even hostility) toward others but through the creation of complex customs and institutions that instill values and habits including altruism and selfishness. The trick in using sociobiology to make sense of parental behavior therefore lies in identifying the competing tendencies and the possible tradeoffs among them.

[Carbone and Cahn] show the complexity of trying to figure out, based on sociobiology's insights, available empirical evidence and efforts to predict the impact of societal norms on human behavior—what parentage-defining policies will maximize the likelihood of providing children with nurturing parents.

Biology may matter. Human beings may be genetically programmed to prefer their genetic offspring over other children. But factors other than biology also matter in shaping parenting desires and capacities. Social conditioning has a huge impact. Moreover, it seems likely that we would maximize human happiness if we were to shape our culture in ways that reduced rather than reinforced any natural tendency to prefer our genetic relatives over others.

Increasingly, even sociobiologists who promote the biological favoritism thesis admit and even assert that the "is" is not the same as the "ought," that culture matters, that humans are different from other animals, and that part of the point of human existence is to overcome nature. Dawkins writes that human beings have the capacity to defy their genetic programming and to cultivate altruism deliberately. [Author] Robert Wright argues that an important point of understanding our genetic nature is to figure out how to move beyond it towards conscience, sympathy, and love for unrelated others.

> "The major impact of divorce on the child is in adulthood, when the man-woman relationship moves center stage."

# Divorce Has a Lasting Negative Impact

*Judith Wallerstein*

*Judith Wallerstein is a family researcher and the author of a landmark study that presented the long-term negative effects of divorce on children. For thirty years, she studied six thousand children of divorce, some of them over a twenty-five year period in their lives. The following viewpoint appears in the anthology,* Marriage—Just a Piece of Paper? *In it, the author claims that although divorce might represent significant improvements in the lives of the adults who undergo it, divorce immediately upsets the lives of children from preschool through high school, with consequences that last into adulthood.*

As you read, consider the following questions:

1. What were some unintended consequences of the passage of the "no-fault" divorce law in California in 1969?

Judith Wallerstein, "What about the Children?" *Marriage—Just a Piece of Paper?* Edited by Katherine Anderson, Don Browning, and Brian Boyer. Grand Rapids, MI: William B. Eerdmans Publishing Co., 2002, pp. 92–105. Copyright © 2002 The University of Chicago. Reproduced by permission.

2. In what ways does divorce contribute to "diminished parenting"?

3. What are some ways that the impact of divorce influences the structure and behavior of a child's adult life?

In 1969, California, which is a flagship state in family law, passed the first no-fault divorce law. It was developed out of a consortium of the right and the left. The law was written as a result of several task forces the last one headed by a woman who was a leading feminist and law professor, and it was signed by [Governor] Ronald Reagan. It was a day of great celebration in California because it would end trouble in marriage: People who had made a mistake could leave the marriage. They would obviously agree quietly and happily. Remarkably, there was no consideration, despite all the task forces, about how this major piece of family legislation would impact on children. You know, I can't believe it. It's a major part of history that shows how little we consider the impact of so much of legislation and so much of social change on the family and especially on children, who unfortunately don't vote. . . .

I happened to come to California at that historic time, where I was in a ringside seat at a community mental health center. We got many telephone calls all of a sudden from agitated parents saying, "What am I going to do about my children? My husband and I have divorced, or are divorcing, and the children are aggressive. They're crying. They're acting up. They're not going to sleep. They're behaving in ways I've never seen before." The nursery school teacher called saying, "We don't know what to do." The calls came around preschool children. We looked at each other. It was a highly trained professional staff. I went to the library, being a scholar at heart, and I discovered that, lo and behold, there was no research, none, on the impact of divorce on children, despite, and I say ironically, our major efforts to change the family. We hadn't looked at this.

We saw children who were very frightened. There were sleep disturbances. Children who had never been particularly aggressive in elementary school and in preschool were hitting other children. The nursery school teachers and the elementary school teachers are saying these kids are out of control, and the only change that occurred in their lives had been the divorce of their parents. . . .

## Divorce Makes Children Insecure

The children had a sense of loss, and anger at their parents. Their great fear was that they would be abandoned. I mean, this is a wealthy country. We had largely middle-class children who had never been hungry in their lives who were suddenly afraid that they would starve to death, that they would wake up in the morning and there would be nobody to take care of them. They were overwhelmed with frightening fantasies that had to do with the fear that the scaffolding of their lives was collapsing under them.

So we decided to take children aged three to sixteen, and we went back a year later. Since I was very much in accord with community opinion, I had no reason to doubt it. I thought everything would be fine. Okay, so the kids were upset, but they would be over with it. I mean, a year is a long time in the life of a four year old. It's 25 percent of her life, right?

Lo and behold, the children were worse. Parents were more worried. There were economic problems which were beginning to surface which people hadn't expected. Child support wasn't paid automatically. Parent-child relationships changed a lot. . . .

This one little girl told me that at age four she used to sit outside the bathroom door, which her mother would lock.

Her mother would be in there studying for an exam that she was going to have the next day. The only peace and quiet the mom could have from the three children would be locking herself in the bathroom. The child would sit cross-legged outside the bathroom door, waiting for the mother to come out. This was a child who had been the center of her mother's life and the father's life. The father had an economic crisis. He disappeared, really, in great crisis, and in great trouble. The mom was out working during the day and going to school at night. When I saw the little girl, she said to me, "I'm looking for a mommy. I need a new mommy."

That's a difference in a child's life. That is different. Is it poor parenting? I hate to call that poor parenting. It's diminished parenting. It's tragically diminished parenting. But this is clearly a mother and a father who under other circumstances were both devoted to this child. So it's a crisis in the parents' lives. It's not an easy-come, easy-go decision, which then reverberates into the child's life. It is experienced by the child as an abandonment. . . .

## It's Not Just Childhood

The major impact of divorce is really in adulthood. The early reaction is very painful, but it fades after a few years if the family is reasonably functioning. The average number of years it takes is about three and a half or four years, something like that. But the major impact of divorce on the child is in adulthood, when the man-woman relationship moves center stage.

Divorce isn't any old crisis. It's not a tornado. It's not a death in the family. It's a very specific crisis of the breakdown of the relationship between the main man and the main woman in the child's life. Children, I've come to the conclusion, identify not only with their mom and their dad as people, as we've generally accepted, but they clearly internalize the relationship between them. They spend all their time observing the relationship between them. I know all the details, espe-

## Significance of Trends in Family Structure

Both the number and the type of parents (i.e. biological, step) in a child's household can have strong effects on their well-being. Single-parent families tend to have much lower incomes than do two-parent families, but research indicates that the income differential accounts for only about one-half of the negative effects of parent absence on many areas of child and youth well-being, including health, educational attainment and assessment, behavior problems and psychological well-being. . . .

From 1970 to 1996, the percentage of all children under age 18 who were living with two married parents decreased steadily from 85 percent to 68 percent. The percentage stabilized during the late 1990s, and was at 67 percent in 2005.

Since 1970, the percentage of children living in mother-only families has increased from 11 percent to 24 percent in 1997 and was at 23 percent in 2005. Between 1970 and 2005, the percentage of children living in father-only families increased from 1 percent to 5 percent. The percentage living without either parent (with other relatives or with non-relatives) rose slightly from 3 percent to 5 percent.

In 2005, 6 percent of all children lived in the home of their grandparents. In more than half of these families, however, one or both parents were also present.

*"Family Structure,"*
*Child Trends Data Bank, 2006,*
*www.childtrendsdatabank.org.*

cially from the children in the intact families that I interviewed, about how Mom and Dad get along. Do they kiss each other? Does he pinch her? Do they dance? Are they angry? Do they talk? Do they fight in the open? Do they fight behind closed doors? When the bedroom door closes, does that mean they are fighting? Or are they making love? So that's a tremendous source of knowledge for any growing child. They spend their whole life studying that.

There is nothing they study in school that they look at as carefully as they do the man-woman relationship in their family. Their parents may have successfully decided to divorce, it may have been the best decision of their lives. From the child's perspective, they failed. It's very hard for grown-ups to realize. It doesn't mean they've failed, it means from their child's perspective they failed. From their child's perspective they failed to keep it together. She failed to keep the man; he failed to keep the lady. And they failed in their child's view at one of the major tasks of life and, for the young adult's view, the major task at that point.

They have trouble in their third decade of life, in their twenties, in knowing what they are looking for in a man or a woman, in believing that they can keep it together, in believing that they can have a lasting relationship. Their fear of failure is very powerful—as powerful (and this is their conflict) as their intense wish to do better than their parents did.

## "I Am Not My Parents"

The tremendous inner conflict does and doesn't get resolved. This is their task in their twenties. They have to take that inner image of a failed man-woman relationship and disassociate themselves from it and give themselves another shot. They say, "I'm going to do it my way. I'm not my mom. I'm not my dad. I'm me." They acquire hope and confidence also from other arenas in their lives. So they have to learn from their own experience.

They are remarkable, really, in that they do for themselves what children really have a right to expect from their parents. They create their own morality. As one young person said to me, "Both my parents lied and cheated. I decided I'm never going to lie." They create their own morality, and many of them have a really very high morality. As one young woman said to me, "Sometimes I feel that I was brought up on a desert island. The idea of sex and love and intimacy all together is a strange idea to me. The guys I have a good time with, I really don't even like." But they put it together by the time they're thirty, thirty-one, or thirty-two. It takes them longer to grow up. They do it themselves, or it's the luck of the draw. They meet somebody. People change a lot in adulthood. They just don't grow up in childhood.

## Always Afraid of Loss

The other residue in adulthood, which surprised me, because I didn't expect it, is the fact that almost all, and I say this very carefully, of the children of divorce, as adults, suffered with a residue of symptoms in which they were afraid that disaster would strike suddenly, unaware. The happier they were, the better their life, the better their job, the better their love life, the better their relationship, the better their children, the more frightened they became that they would lose it.

I think this is clearly related to what I said about the fact that so few of them expected the divorce when it happened. From their point of view, everything was going well and BOOM—the floor fell out from under them. We always tell everybody lightning doesn't strike twice because profoundly in our heart, we know it strikes twice. We all believe it strikes twice, so we reassure ourselves with false reassurances, and this is the fear of lightning striking twice.

Now, I'm not sure it ever goes away, in the same way that I'm not sure that a child of divorce ever fully trusts another person. I hate to say this, but I think it is true. I'm not sure a child of divorce ever fully trusts that another person will be there for them, will love them, will be dependable and will love them forever, whatever forever consists of. In some corner of their heart, there is the fear that that person won't be there in the morning, either will betray them or will abandon them. . . .

## Parents' and Children's Needs Diverge

We didn't realize that divorce doesn't rescue children. Divorce is a good thing for adults. For a lot of adults, it changes their lives very much for the better. But except in violence, and not always in violence, divorce doesn't rescue children from the loneliness and unhappiness of a marriage that they usually don't experience.

Divorce in the life of a child is entirely different than in the life of an adult. For an adult, it is a remedy. It brings a bad chapter of my life to an end and opens the door, and hopefully, with any luck, I'll do it better next time around. Doesn't always work, but then life doesn't always work out. But for the child, it's not a remedy, it's the loss of the family, and there is no substitute for that family that's lost.

> "Much of the current writing about divorce, both popular and academic, has exaggerated its negative effects and ignored its sometimes considerable positive effects."

# Divorce Does Not Have a Lasting Negative Impact

*Karen S. Peterson*

*Karen S. Peterson is a journalist who writes on the topics of marriage, family, and current topics in American life. The following viewpoint details the findings of a long-term study by respected family researcher, E. Mavis Hetherington. After tracking thousands of children of divorce over the course of several decades, Dr. Hetherington concluded that most children are not permanently harmed when their parents split up. Although divorce begins a difficult time in anyone's life, with supportive parents, most children recover and go on to lead happy, productive lives.*

As you read, consider the following questions:

1. Approximately how long does it take before children begin to "function reasonably" again after their parents' divorce?

Karen S. Peterson, "Divorce Need Not End in Disaster," *USA Today* (online edition), January 13, 2002, www.usatoday.com.

2. What aspects of Hetherington's research lend credibility to her findings and respect from her peers?

3. Regardless of how well children bounce back after divorce, what negative effects of divorce did Hetherington document?

A new, book-length study . . . says that the negative impact of divorce on both children and parents has been exaggerated and that only about one-fifth of youngsters experience any long-term damage after their parents break up. One of the most comprehensive studies of divorce to date, the research will bring balm to the souls of parents who have chosen to end their marriages. It probably also will incense those who see divorce as undermining American society.

After studying almost 1,400 families and more than 2,500 children—some of them for three decades—trailblazing researcher E. Mavis Hetherington finds that about 75% to 80% of children from divorced homes are "coping reasonably well and functioning in the normal range." Eventually they are able to adapt to their new lives.

About 70% of their parents are leading lives that range from "good enough"—the divorce was "like a speed bump in the road"—to "enhanced," living lives better than those they had before the divorce.

About 70% of kids in stepfamilies are "pretty happy," Hetherington says. And 40% of couples in stepfamilies were able to build "stable, reasonably satisfying marriages." . . .

## A Clear Objective View

Hetherington is publishing her relatively positive findings in *For Better or For Worse: Divorce Reconsidered.* Her co-author is journalist John Kelly. The summation of her life's work is long awaited by polarized academics—and aimed at clearing up confusion among moms and dads worried about divorce.

## Divorce Actually Helps Some Girls in School

Contrary to the expectation that marriage is always good for children while divorce is bad, [a University of Florida] study found that the schoolwork of girls whose parents split up is better than that of girls who live with a mom and dad who don't get along. . . .

In the study, girls between first- and 10th-grades whose parents divorced scored an average of slightly more than eight points higher on standardized reading and mathematics tests than girls whose parents filed for divorce but later requested the case be dismissed. These differences persisted four years after the divorce.

*Cathy Keen, "UF Study: Girls Perform Better on Tests when Feuding Parents Divorce," University of Florida News, September 7, 2006, http://news.ufl.edu.*

Much of the current writing about divorce both popular and academic, "has exaggerated its negative effects and ignored its sometimes considerable positive effects," Hetherington writes.

Ending a marriage, she says, "is an experience that for most people is challenging and painful. But it is also a window of opportunity to build a new and better life."

## A Summary of Findings

Hetherington, whose research methods are regarded by her peers as the gold standard, is professor emeritus in the department of psychology at the University of Virginia. She writes:

The vast majority of children within two years after their parents' divorce "are beginning to function reasonably well again."

Most young adults from divorced families were "behaving the way young adults were supposed to behave, choosing careers, developing permanent relationships, ably going about the central tasks of young adulthood."

For every young adult from a divorced family that is having social, emotional or psychological problems, . . . others are functioning well. Most divorced women "manage to provide the support, sensitivity and engagement their children need for normal development." Single moms "deserve a prize" for their efforts, she says. "Many of them are real heroes."

Women tend to come out of divorce better than men, despite the financial dilemmas many experience. "A subset of our women and girls turned out to be more competent, able people than if they had stayed in unhappy family situations."

## The Public Conversation about Divorce

Hetherington's new book comes at a pivotal time. The divorce rate actually has dropped slightly in the 1990s, from a high of more than 50% of new marriages ending in divorce to about 43% currently. But for most experts, the numbers still are unacceptably high.

Just how much damage divorce does to kids is a real hot-button topic. Hetherington's findings contradict those of several renowned experts who say the children are at risk for a variety of difficulties, including dropping out of school, emotional problems, substance abuse, having babies out of wedlock and having their own marriages end in divorce.

Over the past decade, researchers highlighting such results have dominated the public deliberations, leading some state legislatures to debate changes in divorce laws.

Hetherington now steps in, hoping to alter the national dialogue. The country has been so caught up in believing that the long-term effects of divorce are inevitably harmful that it is almost becoming a self-fulfilling prophecy, Hetherington says. "I think it is really important to emphasize that most do cope and go on to have a reasonably happy or sometimes very happy life," she says.

She adds a caveat. To ensure an emotionally healthy youngster, "there must be a competent, caring parent," she says.

## Hetherington's Research Methods

The 75-year-old developmental psychologist—she volunteers her age—does have credentials. She invented many of the in-depth tools now commonly used to measure well-being in families, producing a nuanced look at what happens in divorce. And she has a control group of intact families for much of her work, so she can make comparisons with the normal troubles non-divorced families encounter.

That control group, the size of her sample, the length of time she has gathered data and the thoroughness of her work awe her peers. "She is the leading social scientist who studies the effects of divorce on children," says Andrew Cherlin, a sociologist at Johns Hopkins University in Baltimore. "She was the pioneer in her field, and we have all followed in her wake. She was the first serious researcher to do excellent, rigorous studies of children and families. Everyone has read her work and learned from it."

Family historian Stephanie Coontz, co-chairman of the Council on Contemporary Families, says Hetherington is "the perfectly balanced scholar. She is absolutely respected among her peers. Her advice is as good as you are going to get."

## Plenty of Drawbacks

Seated in her 100-year-old home, a renovated schoolhouse overlooking the Blue Ridge mountains, Hetherington elaborates on her incendiary goal: altering the national debate. Her voice takes on a slightly sharp edge. She does not believe that divorce is all right. "I am saying it is painful," she says.

But it is also true that the disastrous results of splitting up have been exaggerated for both children and parents. A lot of

149

people believe that "if you have gone through a divorce, you are inflicting a terminal disease on your children," she says.

Few criticize Hetherington outright. But even as many tip their hats to her, the disapproving already are lining up.

David Blankenhorn, one skeptic, is the author of *Fatherless America* and a leader of the growing "marriage movement," which seeks to reduce the number of marriages that end in divorce.

Hetherington's book will stoke "a sort of backlash," Blankenhorn says. "We have made so much progress in the last 10 years in what I would call realism about divorce. Reputable scholars have led a trend away from a kind of 'happy talk' approach to divorce. Even the title of her book says something: that we are reconsidering divorce, the fact that divorce is harmful to children." He takes issue with those like Hetherington who believe, he says, that "we shouldn't worry so much" or that "the kids will be fine."

Judith Wallerstein, a rival doyenne of family research, is ready to do battle with Hetherington. In 1989, Wallerstein's *Second Chances* became a surprise bestseller. While some academics faulted the small size her sample (about 60 families), some of her research methods and her sweeping generalizations, the public noticed her results. Parents worried about what the children of divorce said, that while splitting up might be seen as a second change for happiness by adults, it is not by their kids.

## The Problems of Divorce

Wallerstein found that children of divorce lack role models for healthy marriages, have a longer adolescence as they help heal wounded parents, have less of a chance at college, greater substance-abuse problems, less competence in social relationships and often difficulty bonding in stepfamilies. . . .

When one goes deeper into Hetherington's wide-ranging book, some alarming findings do emerge:

- 70% of young people from divorced families see divorce as an acceptable solution, even if children are present. Marriage is forever "if things work out." Only 40% from intact families do.

- Fewer than 20% of young adult stepchildren feel close to their stepmoms. The divorce rate in remarriages is greater than those in first marriages, frequently because the stepmother is unpopular: She is often caught in the middle, expected to be nurturer of sometimes difficult and suspicious children.

- Men and boys adjust emotionally less well after a divorce in the family than women and girls. Divorced men do poorly alone and remarry quickly, while boys become challenges to the single moms they tend to live with, often losing touch with dads.

## The Complete Picture

Still, most children of divorce make it through. Rather than thinking about "the inevitability of any one kind of outcome of divorce," Hetherington hopes readers think about the "diversity of outcomes. What is striking is that we go from those who are totally defeated, mired in depression and poverty, to these ebullient, happy, satisfied people making wonderful contributions to their families and society.". . .

Hetherington has been married 46 years and has three grown sons and three grandchildren. Neither she nor her sons have ever been divorced.

And she would like to make one thing perfectly clear. "The last thing I want to do is sound like I am recommending divorce. I am not pro-divorce. I think people should work harder on their marriages and be better prepared when they go in and more willing to weather out the rough spots and support each other."

But divorce, she says, "is a legitimate decision. If children are in marriages with parents who are contemptuous of each other, not even with overt conflict, but just sneering and subtle putdowns that erode the partner's self-esteem, that is very bad for kids."

# Periodical Bibliography

*The following articles have been selected to supplement the diverse views presented in this chapter.*

James Bogle — "Do the Courts Regard Fathers as Redundant?" *National Observer*, Summer 2005.

Amy Johnson Conner — "Parental Alienation: The Latest Weapon in Nasty Divorces," *Journal Record* (Oklahoma City, OK), April 26, 2007.

Mary Eberstadt — "Revenge of the Rugrats: A New Generation Weighs in on Divorce," *Weekly Standard*, October 10, 2005.

Karen Fanning — "Step by Step: Fifty Percent of Kids in the United States Live in Stepfamilies," *Scholastic Choices*, September 2005.

Shirley Henderson — "The Good Stepmother: As African-Americans Form More Stepfamilies, the Role of the New Woman Has Become More Prominent," *Ebony*, May 2006.

Carl Jones — "State Justices Rule Divorced Man Must Support Child He Didn't Father," *Palm Beach Daily Business Review*, February 2, 2007.

Joanne Malino — "How I Survived My Parents' Divorce," *Cosmo-Girl!* August 2006.

Jill Miller — "Step-Father Can Seek Custody of Step-Daughter," *Daily Record* (Rochester, NY), September 21, 2004.

Tim Stafford — "Can This Institution Be Saved? A Curious Alliance of Helping Professionals Is Working to Rebuild Marriage in a Culture of Divorce," *Christianity Today*, November 2004.

*Women's Health Weekly* — "Girls Living with Alcoholic Stepfather Have More Behavior Problems than Boys," June 10, 2004.

Cathy Young — "Parent Trap: Are False Abuse Charges a Common Tactic in Custody Battles?" *Reason*, December 2006.

# CHAPTER 4

# Should Government Make Policies Regarding Families?

# Chapter Preface

The ideal of the common good entails all members of a community making contributions and sacrifices so that every person enjoys the same social benefits. It is an ideal that is unobjectionable in theory but that can become problematic in practice, mostly because the common good is a nebulous term that means different things to different people. Does it refer merely to providing food and shelter for all? Should every child get a government-funded education? Does a community need reliable roads and clean water? Must access to comprehensive health care be guaranteed to every member of society? Should wealthier citizens contribute money in the form of taxes to provide these items for people who cannot afford to buy them?

Discussions on this topic often include references to the social contract—a tacit understanding among a group of people that it is beneficial to give up some personal liberties for the sake of a harmonious, all-inclusive social order and that government representatives are elected for the purpose of preserving this order. In contrast to the proponents of the social contract are the proponents of natural rights—people who believe that humans should only be governed by their conscience, that the practice of acting in one's own self-interest ultimately benefits the lives of everyone. Behaviors that are bad for society are also bad for individuals, who will therefore not engage in them for reasons of self-preservation.

Modern nations create governments along a spectrum defined on one end by a social contract of shared and mutual responsibility and at on the other end by individual autonomy and natural rights. Trying to embody both philosophies creates conflict in the United States, which incorporated both values. Americans revered ideas of the self-made man, characters who attained greatness by their own grit and determination; simultaneously, Americans subscribed to the idea that the stronger among them should look out for those less fortunate. Conflicted over these two values, Americans empower government to fund social programs but object when those programs become expensive and ask for more funds.

Government policy towards families, especially families with minor children, exists in this state of contrary values. Should parents be solely responsible for the welfare of their children, or should government intervene to protect children's rights and help prepare them for their role as future citizens? Is it in someone's best interest to care about what happens to a stranger's child in another state? For a variety of reasons, many Westernized nations in the early 2000s experienced dramatic reductions in fertility rates; adults are no longer leaving enough children behind to replace them. These future population declines mean that there will be fewer people to govern (and take care of), and there will be fewer active contributors to the national economy. If the health of the community at large suffers, will it have any effect on the opportunities for individual happiness?

Nations and their governments struggle to find a balance between personal freedom and obligations to others, to find a compromise between private gain and the common good. The authors in the following chapter tackle three issues related to public policy towards families, the most personal and private institution of all.

*"Marriage is an important public health and safety issue. It is a legitimate concern of the state, and we should make every effort to promote the institution."*

# Married People Should Have Unique Legal Privileges

*Steven L. Nock*

*Steven Nock is a professor of sociology at the University of Virginia. His research has investigated issues of privacy, cohabitation, commitment, divorce, and marriage; he focuses on how public policy affects American families. The following viewpoint appears in the book,* Revitalizing the Institution of Marriage for the Twenty-First Century. *In it, the author argues that the government should establish legal and economic privileges for people who get married because marriage is beneficial to society. Although this action would mean that married people and single people are treated differently, promoting marriage improves the quality of life of every American.*

As you read, consider the following questions:

1. How does getting married tend to improve the life of the adult who does so?
2. How does the de-institutionalizing of marriage contribute to the attitude of egalitarianism in modern society?
3. What specific benefits to society does marriage provide?

There are those who would argue that married people should be viewed as no different from unmarried people. According to this view, the rights and responsibilities of all people should be equal. Marriage should not be privileged in law or elsewhere. To confer such a privilege, some believe, will perpetuate invidious distinctions between the married and the unmarried. Indeed, there is also much evidence that marriage is being de-institutionalized, in law most obviously, but also in popular culture. Cohabitation is no longer stigmatized. Unmarried childbearing, likewise, is increasingly common and essentially indistinguishable in law from married childbearing. . . .

Marriage produces measurable and significant benefits for the adults involved. Married people are healthier, happier, more successful, and more productive. Married people are more generous to others and more likely to join organizations devoted to community improvement. Married individuals continue to benefit from the assumptions made about them. Married men, especially, are viewed as more mature, independent, and trustworthy than their unmarried counterparts. Regardless of the details of the particular relationship involved, married men and women derive significant benefits from their status. Were this not so, cohabiting individuals would be more similar to married people. A decade of research has convincingly shown this to be not so.

There is also unequivocal evidence that children fare better in marriages than in other forms of relationships. Whether a child is born to an unmarried woman, or is the product of di-

## What Is the Healthy Marriage Promotion Initiative?

Marriage classes ... these are going on all over the country with federal funding support, teaching marriage cultivation and preservation to low-income couples.

The concept of promoting strong marriages as a way to fight poverty was listed as one of the goals of welfare reform legislation—the Personal Responsibility and Work Opportunity Reconciliation Act of 1996—signed into law by former President Bill Clinton.

But it wasn't until the passage of the 2006 deficit-reduction bill that Congress went beyond words, approving a $750 million, five-year plan to encourage healthy marriage and fatherhood. The measure includes $100 million a year for marriage-related programs.

Supporters believe that marriage benefits society as a whole because married couples tend to be better off and enjoy more financial stability, and because children in two-parent families fare better by some measures than those in single-parent families.

*Roshin Mathew, "Marriage: An Anti-Child-Poverty Program,"*
*Connect for Kids, July 24, 2006, www.connectforkids.org.*

vorce, the long-term consequences are comparable. Such children are less successful as adults, have higher rates of depression and other psychological disorders, and are more likely to experience poverty and divorce. They complete fewer years of schooling and drop out of school more often than children from married households.

Finally, there is the obvious yet unknown collective cost we pay, as a society, for the de-institutionalization of marriage. The microeconomic costs are already well known: higher rates of poverty, welfare receipt, Medicaid, public assistance, hospital admissions, suicide, chronic and acute illnesses, and accidents, and lower productivity and earnings. If we were able to estimate the macroeconomic costs of divorce, unmarried childbearing, and lower marriage rates, we would surely discover that we pay an enormous price for the retreat from marriage. Seen from this perspective, marriage is an important public health and safety issue. It is a legitimate concern of the state, and we should make every effort to promote the institution. . . .

## Public Issues Surrounding Marriage

The view of marriage as a private contract negotiated by the spouses themselves is driven, in part, by a compassionate concern that traditional marriage denied women equal protection in law. The de-institutionalization of marriage is also a reflection of an egalitarian ethic that views unmarried people as no less entitled to the prerogatives of civic life than husbands and wives. In short, the move to de-institutionalize marriage is a practical consequence of the concern over equal protection.

Consider only a few of the vexing questions we now face as we consider such moral issues. Should unmarried people enjoy the same legal and social privileges granted to married adults? Should all zoning and housing laws be neutral with respect to marital status? Should children born to unmarried parents be treated the same as those born into a marriage? Should homosexuals be allowed to marry? Should welfare benefits be the same for married and unmarried parents? Should married people pay the same federal and state taxes as unmarried people? Should children conceived in vitro or by artificial insemination and born to a surrogate mother be treated the same as those conceived, gestated, and born in marriage? There are strong egalitarian arguments in support of each position. At the same time, each idea amounts to a significant challenge to traditional assumptions embodied in the social institution of marriage.

Is it possible to grant all individuals equal standing in law without de-institutionalizing marriage? In fact, it is not. But the institution of marriage is much more than law. Indeed, for most of human history, marriage was totally unregulated by the state. Today, for almost all spouses, law assumes psychological significance in marriage only when the relationship ends in divorce. Thus, whether or not marriage is distinguished from other forms of intimate relationships in law is unlikely to affect the way people view marriage as a social institution—at least not immediately. However, the symbolic effect of de-institutionalizing legal marriage will gradually erode the social distinctions associated with marriage. Law may not be an important cause of behavior in the short term, but it is quite important in symbolizing and codifying values. For that reason, I believe the current legal project to de-institutionalize marriage is unwise.

## Justifying Preferential Treatment

How then are we to justify any legal distinction between married and unmarried people? There are two simple answers to this question. First, we must recognize the collective benefits all people enjoy because couples get married. I suggest that we begin with significant macroeconomic benefits (e.g., lower rates of poverty, higher adult productivity, healthier and better educated children). Second, we must recognize that married people deserve (in a moral sense) certain legal privileges in return for the sacrifices they make in their personal lives. Such legal benefits are intended to symbolize the value Americans place on marriage.

Married people are justifiably entitled to different treatment in law because marriage requires different behaviors. At a minimum, married people voluntarily limit their personal autonomy in many ways. The soft boundaries that define the institution of marriage are, essentially, self-imposed limits on behavior, or sacrifices of personal autonomy. These sacrifices are sufficient grounds for differential treatment in law. They may be regarded as a strong form of social control, voluntarily accepted by most spouses as part of their marriage vows. Unless we discover an equally effective and economical form of social control, and until we are willing to accept the collective costs of doing so, we should be cautious of de-institutionalizing marriage.

I believe it is justifiable to grant marriage legal and social privileges. I believe the collective benefits of marriage justify such a distinction. Indeed, those whose thoughts and actions influence public opinion and law have an obligation to promote marriage in this way. Presumably, most Americans accept the legal and economic privileges that are presently granted by state and federal governments to those who own their homes, to those who send their children to college, to those who save for their retirement, and those who donate to charities, to mention only a few examples. Marriage is no less beneficial to the collective health of our society than an of these other actions. Indeed, it is more so.

VIEWPOINT

*"The great majority of singles in this country can legitimately argue that, at least for tax purposes, they are treated like second-class citizens."*

# Married People Should Not Have Unique Legal Privileges

*John O. Fox*

*John Fox teaches tax policy at Mount Holyoke College. In the following viewpoint, he presents the hypothetical case of a single person at the poverty level paying income taxes to the same scenario for a married couple with two children at the poverty level. Despite public outcry about a "marriage penalty" in the income tax code, the author argues that it is really single people who are hurt the most. He concludes by providing suggestions for how Congress could change the tax code in order to make it fair to all citizens, regardless of marital status.*

As you read, consider the following questions:

1. Why does the author say that there is a "singles penalty" in the income tax system?
2. What is the difference between the minimum income a single person must earn and the minimum combined income a married couple must earn before paying taxes?

John O. Fox, "For Singles, April Really Is the Cruelest Month," *The Washington Post*, April 11, 2004, p. B1. Copyright © 2004 Washington Post. Reproduced by permission of the author.

3. Why is it easier for married people (who earn the minimum amount to pay income taxes) to live well than it is for single people?

They're the buzzwords in Washington these days: "marriage" and "family values." Of course, we're having a little disagreement over how to define them, what with President Bush's marriage initiative and the proposal for a constitutional amendment to define the institution pitted against the fight for same-sex marriages. Still, underlying these divisions is the belief among all groups that family matters. And so Congress strives, in the tax laws, to promote family values.

Lost in the conversation, meanwhile, is any mention of "singles values." But the choice to be single, whether temporary or permanent, should be accorded the same dignity as the choice to marry, shouldn't it? Including under our tax laws. You'd think that Congress, above all, would be sensitive to the interests of singles, because there are so many of them—every year, there are more single income tax returns filed than joint ones (58 million vs. 51 million in 2001). But if you viewed single people solely by the way Congress chooses to tax most of them, you might think they were, well, almost un-American. The way they're treated isn't fair, and it should change.

## Debunking the "Marriage Penalty"

You've all heard about the tax system's so-called marriage penalty, which discourages a couple with good incomes from marrying because their combined income taxes would be greater than if they remained single. Congress heard so much about it that, through legislation in 2001 and 2003, it addressed that problem for most couples by increasing their standard deduction and broadening their tax brackets. But a great injustice remains in our tax system: the "singles penalty." The annual income tax deadline arrives this week, and there's no getting around it—most of us who are married and also have young kids are going to fare a lot better than most of those who haven't tied the knot or had any children.

Don't know anything about this? Well, you should, especially if you are among those single taxpayers who don't itemize their deductions. That's roughly 80 percent of all singles—a total of about 48 million individuals, if you're counting. While the singles penalty is harshest on lower- and moderate-income earners, it affects all 48 million. Here's why.

## Income Tax and Poverty Levels

Consider first our nation's official poverty thresholds. The threshold for single people last year was about $9,600; but single people who claim a standard deduction on their 2003 returns are expected to begin to pay a tax if their income exceeds a mere $9,300—that is, before what they earn has, by the government's own definition, lifted them out of poverty. (The $9,300 tax threshold results from the sum of the personal exemption plus the standard deduction, and the benefit of a small earned income credit.)

So many singles, with modest incomes and modest expenses, depend on the standard deduction—a measly $4,750 in 2003—because it is larger than the sum of what they might itemize. (By contrast, more than half of all joint returns claim itemized deductions.) These singles include many young people and many seniors, but also nearly all people who earn not a whole lot more than the minimum wage and may work two or even three jobs. Many are renters, but Congress prohibits them from deducting any of their rent, even though it often consumes a disproportionate share of their income.

By contrast, Congress views the $19,000 poverty threshold for a working married couple with two young children and typical child care costs as woefully inadequate for purposes of setting their tax threshold. Congress believes that this couple should not begin to pay a penny of income taxes until its in-

## Penalized for Being Single

It's not just the Income Tax Code which treats unmarried Americans unfairly by giving a "marriage bonus" to many couples who file jointly and by taxing domestic partner health benefits but not spousal health benefits.

Social security tax is unfair to singles too. If a single person dies a month before retirement, everything paid into social security is forfeited. But if a married person dies, the surviving spouse gets a survivor benefit.

Federal estate tax should not be forgotten. A married person can leave an unlimited amount of wealth to a surviving spouse, tax free. But a single person with an estate above the exemption level can't leave a bequest to a friend, sibling, or partner without Uncle Sam taking a hefty bite first.

*Thomas F. Coleman, "IRS Digs into Pocket of Low-Income Singles."*
*Unmarried America, 2006, www.unmarriedamerica.org.*

come exceeds $47,700, or about 2 1/2 times its poverty threshold. (To calculate their tax, subtract $12,200 for four personal exemptions and $9,500 for their standard deduction, which leaves $26,000 of taxable income. Taxes tentatively owed: $3,200. Then subtract their tax credits: $2,000 in child credits ($1,000 for each child) and $1,200 in child care credits ($600 for each child), for a total of $3,200. Taxes finally owed: zero.)

That certainly seems reasonable, so single people shouldn't object. But they have every right to ask Congress: Where's your compassion for us?

## Crunching the Numbers

To understand the harshness of the tax threshold imposed on most singles, let's consider one who earns $9,600 and see what it's like for her to try to live on that amount. Well, it isn't really $9,600, because 7.65 percent is withheld for Social Security and Medicare taxes, and, thanks to Congress, she has to pay a small income tax. That leaves $8,835, or about $740 a month.

Our taxpayer—let's call her Meg—lives by herself in an efficiency apartment, doesn't own a car and takes the bus to work and on personal trips. In a typical American city such as Baltimore or Cleveland, she might get that apartment for $350 to $600 a month. Say her rent is $440, which leaves her with $300 to pay for everything else—food, clothing, furniture, household and personal supplies, telephone, utilities, laundry, sales taxes, public transportation, and much more. (Heaven forbid she should actually buy a magazine or go to a movie.) Health insurance alone—she doesn't qualify for Medicaid because she doesn't have a dependent child—would consume much of the $300, so she goes without it and crosses her fingers. It isn't really a choice anyway: Meg runs out of money before she finishes paying her other bills.

Now consider Fran and Bill, a hypothetical married couple with two preschool children. Both work full-time and earn a combined income of $47,700. We'll assume they pay $7,000 for child care ($30 a day, five days a week), and $3,650 in Social Security and Medicare taxes. This leaves about $37,000 (still nearly twice the poverty threshold), or about $3,100 a month, to pay all other expenses. We don't have to elaborate on the details to reach an obvious conclusion: It's a lot easier, given economies of scale, for Fran and Bill to meet their family's basic living expenses on $3,100 a month than it is for Meg to cover her basic living expenses on $740 a month.

Moreover, at their income level, Fran and Bill are more likely than Meg to receive benefits at work, such as paid health insurance premiums or contributions to a retirement plan, none of which count as income on their tax return. This means that their actual income may be greater than $47,700, yet they still don't owe any income tax. Meg probably has only her $9,600 because jobs at her salary level usually offer no benefits.

## Current Tax Disparities Are Unjust

If the scandal here were limited to Meg's income tax of $30 on the difference between her $9,300 tax threshold and the $9,600 poverty threshold, our outrage would be limited. But if Congress is going to recognize, as it should, that a family of four needs income far in excess of its poverty threshold before it can afford to pay an income tax, simple tax justice requires that the same principle be extended to a single person. We may debate the income level at which the change should be made, but I believe the starting point of the discussion should be no less than $1,200 to $1,500 a month ($14,400 to $18,000 a year), from which the federal government will subtract 7.65 percent for Social Security and Medicare taxes. With these new thresholds, we're talking about roughly 8 million to 11 million additional single people who would be protected from being taxed; and in their cases, the tax savings would range from a few hundred dollars to more than $1,000 a year—amounts vitally important to them.

But I would go further. The injustice is not limited to singles who should be spared paying any tax. The initial tax threshold for all singles, including those with higher incomes, should be set so that not one of them pays a tax until their income exceeds a level we regard as necessary to meet basic living expenses. This is what Congress does for that family of four; this is what voters should insist it do for the household of one. Until that time, the great majority of singles in this country can legitimately argued that, at least for tax purposes, they are treated like second-class citizens.

| "Quality preschool provides not only significant benefits for children in both school and life, but tremendous benefits for society."

# Government Should Encourage Preschool Attendance by Young Children

## Susanna Cooper and Kara Dukakis

*Susanna Cooper is the director of Communications for Preschool California, an organization that advocates state-supported preschool programs for every child in the state. Kara Dukakis is the principal policy associate at Children Now, an organization that believes children should be the top public priority. The following viewpoint is from the report* Kids Can't Wait to Learn, *which makes the case for voluntary, universal preschool in California. The authors draw on findings from brain research, preschool results in other states, and economic analysis.*

As you read, consider the following questions:

1. Why is it so important that children have strong reading skills by third grade?

Susanna Cooper and Kara Dukakis, "Proven Benefits: For Education, Business, Public Safety and Society," *Kids Can't Wait to Learn: Achieving Voluntary Preschool for All in California.* Oakland, CA: Preschool California and Children Now, 2004, pp. 11–18. Reproduced with permission.

2. What are three specific ways that preschool benefits a child's entire community?

3. How does preschool attendance benefit middle-class children?

A substantial body of research confirms impressive educational, social and emotional benefits for children who attend quality preschool. That research has convinced a wide array of state and local leaders to call for preschool for all:

- Teachers and school administrators know that children have a better chance of success in school if they have built a strong learning foundation in preschool.

- Business leaders value the high return on investment, and understand that preschool for all helps meet their need for a well-educated workforce.

- Law enforcement officials know that quality early education, and the success in school that follows, is an essential tool to prevent crime and improve public safety in California.

- Parents of hundreds of thousands of California children know that voluntary, quality preschool is critical to their children's success. More than two-thirds of parents of young children believe it is better for children to go to preschool for part of the day than to stay at home full time.

## Longitudinal Research Supports Preschool for All

- The Chicago Child-Parent Center (CPC) Study followed more than 1,500 children over nearly 20 years, documenting the long-term effects of preschool on children's educational and social well-being. The children who attended the CPC preschools were matched to a control group with similar socioeconomic characteristics.

- The Children of the Cost, Quality and Outcomes Study Go to School, conducted in California and three other states around the country by researchers at the University of California, Los Angeles (UCLA) and three other universities, traced the school achievements of 750 children from a variety of backgrounds through second grade. Maternal education and children's gender and ethnicity were accounted for in determining the effects of preschool quality on child outcomes.

- The High/Scope Perry Preschool Study, compared school and other outcomes of low-income 3- and 4-year-olds who attended quality preschool to a similar group of children who did not attend preschool. The study followed participants for more than two decades, with the most recent analysis of participants when they were 27 years old. Study participants were matched based on IQ and then randomly assigned to one of two groups. After ensuring the groups were comparable in terms of socioeconomic status, intelligence, and gender, the two groups were randomly assigned to either the preschool program or the control group, which did not participate in the program.

This research shows that quality preschool provides not only significant benefits for children in both school and life, but tremendous benefits for society.

## Benefits in School

Studies show that children who attend quality preschool perform better in school. Such children are:

- more skilled at reading and math, as demonstrated on standardized tests;

- less likely to be placed in special education,

- less likely to be held back a grade;

- better behaved in class; and

- more likely to graduate from high school.

By the end of third grade, the path to school success or failure has been charted for many children, largely depending on their ability to read. Up until third grade, children learn to read. But from third grade on, they will need to read to learn. Those who have not learned efficient reading skills may be blocked from every other subject in school. That's why quality preschool—which lays a strong foundation for literacy is so critical.

Children in quality preschool programs score higher on standardized tests of reading and math than children who are not enrolled in such programs. This gives children who have attended quality preschool an advantage over others during their K-12 years.

- Children in the High/Scope Perry Preschool program scored significantly higher on intellectual and language tests in elementary school than children who did not participate in the program. Participants continued to outscore their peers on a school achievement test given at age 14 and on general literacy tests at age 27.

- Children who participated in the Chicago Child-Parent Centers (CPC) received higher average scores on reading and math tests during elementary school and were more likely to pass a standardized test of math and language arts in eighth grade than children who did not participate in the CPC program.

- The Children of the Cost, Quality and Outcomes Study Go to School found a strong connection between the quality of early care and children's performance on math and reading tests. From preschool through the second grade, when the study ended, children in higher quality settings, much like those called for in a preschool-for-all system, had higher language scores and better math skills.

Good preschool programs are like preventive medicine: They identify challenges early on, before they become full-blown problems. Research shows that children who attend quality preschool programs are significantly less likely to be placed in special education programs than those who do not attend such programs:

- In the Chicago Child-Parent Center (CPC) study, children who participated in CPC programs were nearly half as likely to be placed in special education as non-CPC participants.

- The High/Scope Perry Preschool Study found similar results. Children who attended the Perry Preschool program were half as likely to spend time in special education programs compared to children who did not attend preschool.

## Early Screening, Early Intervention

Conservative estimates indicate that at least 124,000 California children younger than age 5 have or will develop a disability, or mental or behavior disorder. With thorough screening and appropriate intervention, early identification of problems can make a big difference. According to some estimates, if good screening tools are used, 75% of children with special needs can be identified. Once identified, focused early intervention can reduce the need for ongoing special education services.

Quality preschool programs provide a timely opportunity for early identification. Research shows that children who attend quality preschool programs are significantly less likely to be placed in special education programs than those who do not attend such programs. Studies also show that focused preschool services for children with special needs produce signifi-

# Preschool Curriculum Guide

Colors and Shapes

- Recognizes and names primary colors.

- Recognizes circles.

- Recognizes rectangles.

- Matches shapes or objects based on shape.

- Copies shapes.

Numbers

- Counts orally through 10.

- Counts objects in one-to-one correspondence.

- Understands empty and full.

- Understands more and less.

Reading Readiness

- Knows what a letter is.

- Repeats a sentence of 6-8 words.

- Completes incomplete sentence with proper word.

- Understands that print carries a message.

- Identifies own first name in manuscript.

- Prints own first name.

*Preschool Curriculum Guide,*
*World Book Encyclopedia and Learning Resources, 2007,*
*www.worldbook.com.*

cant academic, social and economic benefits, as well as savings to society. Providing access to quality preschool for children with special needs can help support their development and prepare them for a successful transition to kindergarten and beyond.

Children who participate in quality preschool programs are also less likely to be held back in school than children who do not participate in quality preschool: In the Chicago Child-Parent Center study, children who did not attend the CPC program were 67% more likely to be held back in school than those who participated in the program.

Educational achievement and social success hinge on positive behavior in the classroom; and children who attend quality preschool programs behave better in class.

- A study of North Carolina's Smart Start preschool program showed that children who participated in the program were less likely to have behavioral problems than children who did not attend such programs.

- The Cost, Quality and Outcomes Study concluded that children in higher quality programs exhibited fewer problem behaviors through second grade, and showed greater sociability at least through kindergarten.

## Higher Rates of High School Graduation

Preschool participants are more likely to finish high school than children who do not have the advantage of preschool, leading to more productive work lives as adults.

- In the High/Scope Perry Preschool study, children who did not participate in the program were a third less likely to graduate from high school than program participants.

- Similarly, children who did not participate in the Chicago Parent-Child Centers were 23% less likely to graduate from high school than program participants.

## Beyond School: The Benefits to Society

The benefits of quality preschool reach far beyond children and their schools, extending to families, neighborhoods and the entire state of California.

Children who have had quality preschool experiences are less likely to become involved in crime.

- Children who did not participate in the High/Scope Perry Preschool program were five times more likely to have multiple arrests by age 27 than children who participated in the program.

- In the Chicago Child-Parent Centers, children who did not participate in the program were 70% more likely to be arrested for a violent crime by the time they reached 18 than children who had participated in the program.

Children who attend quality preschool programs earn higher incomes as adults.

- Children from the High/Scope Perry Preschool Program were more than four times as likely as children who did not attend the program to earn $2,000 or more per month.

Quality preschool decreases the likelihood that participants will become pregnant during their teenage years.

- In the High/Scope Perry Preschool Program study, children who did not attend the program were almost twice as likely to become pregnant as teenagers, compared to those that did attend the program.

## Benefits to Middle-Class Children

Quality preschool programs make dramatic differences in the lives of low-income children, but the benefits don't stop at the poverty line. Quality preschool benefits all children, including those from middle-class backgrounds. Middle-class children need the support that quality preschool provides:

- Studies show that many middle-class children and some upper-middle-class children start kindergarten without a strong learning foundation: A third of middle-class children and a fourth of upper-middle-class children lack key pre-literacy skills when they enter kindergarten.

- Middle-class children also show troubling grade retention and drop-out rates: Nationally, 12% of middle-class children are held back at some point during school, and 11% drop out. Quality preschool improves literacy rates and reduces both high school drop-outs and grade retention.

Studies tell us that the benefits of quality preschool accrue to all who participate:

- The Children of the Cost, Quality and Outcomes Study Go to School, which assessed children across the country from many different backgrounds and income levels, including middle-class children, found that children from all income brackets who were in higher quality care showed better language and math skills and fewer behavior problems through the second grade (age 8), when the study concluded.

- The latest findings from North Carolina's Smart Start Program indicate that program quality positively and significantly influenced children's outcomes, regardless of income and other factors.

- Studies of universal preschool in both Oklahoma and Georgia—programs that serve children from a range of socioeconomic backgrounds—show that all participating children, including middle-class children improved their language and cognitive standardized test scores after a year in the program.

Authoritative research demonstrates the wisdom of investing in quality preschool. Good preschool programs capitalize on a period in children's lives when we stand our best chance of setting them on a path to success, both in school and in life. Research-based evidence demonstrates clear academic and social benefits to children across socioeconomic levels who attend quality preschool programs. And the rest of society also benefits through improvements to the K-12 system, reductions in crime, and greater contributions to the economy.

"*Despite increased enrollment in formal early education programs, student achievement has shown little to no improvement.*"

# Preschool Attendance by Young Children Is Unnecessary

*Darcy Olsen*

*Darcy Olsen is the president of the Goldwater Institute, a think tank that has contributed to many political policy reforms in Arizona. She is an authority on trends in education reforms, economic policy, and government reform. The following viewpoint is in response to political movements to make preschool compulsory. In it, the author presents the findings from research about early childhood education. She concludes that although educationally disadvantaged children do experience some improvement from attending preschool, mainstream children do not.*

As you read, consider the following questions:

    1. About what aspect of early childhood education do government and parents disagree?

Darcy Olsen, *Policy Report #201: Assessing Proposals for Preschool and Kindergarten: Essential Information for Parents, Taxpayers and Policymakers*, Phoenix, AZ: Goldwater Institute, February 8, 2005. Copyright © 2005 All Rights Reserved. Reproduced by permission.

2. What is suspect about the statement that every government dollar invested in full-day kindergarten will save seven dollars in later years?

3. What does the term "fade out" refer to in the context of education?

A rizona's move toward more government preschool and kindergarten programs is not unprecedented. In France, Italy, and the United Kingdom, there is nearly universal enrollment of three- and four-year-olds in center-based institutions. A few states across the country have adopted similar systems. Georgia created the first statewide universal preschool program for four-year-olds in 1993, and Oklahoma, New York, and West Virginia have moved in a similar direction. In 2002, Florida voters adopted a constitutional amendment requiring the state to provide free preschool for every four-year-old child.

Conservative estimates show that Arizona currently [as of 2005] spends more than $410 million annually on various day care and early education programs, including Head Start, preschool, and kindergarten. This estimate does not include funds for tribal and migrant worker programs or multiple funding streams used by school districts to fund all-day kindergarten. As policymakers consider early education proposals, we have the opportunity to examine research on preschool and kindergarten, review experience and findings from domestic programs, and look to international data.

We find strong evidence that the widespread adoption of preschool and full-day kindergarten is unlikely to improve student achievement. For nearly 50 years, local, state, and federal governments and diverse private sources have spent billions of dollars funding early education programs. Some early interventions have had meaningful short-term effects on disadvantaged students' grade-level retention and special education placement. However, the effects of early interventions routinely disappear after children leave the programs. The phenomenon known as "fade out" is important because it means that early schooling may be immaterial to a child's later school performance, or that the current school system as structured is unable to sustain those early gains.

For mainstream children, there is little evidence to support the contention that formal preschool and kindergarten are necessary for school achievement or more advantageous than learning in a traditional setting, and there is some evidence that day care and preschool can be detrimental.

## Attitudes about Early Education

From 1965 to the present day [2005], the United States has undergone a sea change in formal early education. Preschool and kindergarten, which were rarely used, are now the norm. Despite increased enrollment in formal early education programs, student achievement has shown little to no improvement. To the degree that international test data are instructive, America's decentralized early education system is outperforming the European model and excels in equipping students for superior achievement in the elementary years.

Implicit in [Arizona] Governor Napolitano's plan is the presumption that the state should take more responsibility for educating young children. A large majority of "child advocates" envision something similar, with almost seven of 10 saying government policy should move toward a universal, national system similar to those of many European countries. Most parents feel otherwise. More than 70 percent of parents with young children say it is their responsibility to pay the costs of caring for their children, and only one in four would move toward a universal system paid for by the government. Also, a majority of low-income parents (those earning no more than $25,000 per year) believes that bearing the cost is their responsibility and not society's. The public opinion research organization, Public Agenda, reports, "At the most basic level, parents of young children believe that having a full-time parental presence at home is what's best for very young children, and it is what most would prefer for their own family."

## Trends Toward Compulsory Attendance

The Governor attempts to address parents' concerns by saying participation in the programs will be voluntary. Yet it [is] difficult to square that rhetoric with a plan intended to make early education "a lockstep component of public schooling." Today [2005], all 50 states have compulsory attendance laws, applying generally to children between the ages of five and 18, and many policymakers have been forthright in calling for extending compulsory education to preschoolers.

For example, in 2001, District of Columbia councilman Kevin Chavous proposed the "Compulsory School Attendance Amendment Act" to make school compulsory for every preschool-aged child in the nation's capital. The Honorable Zell Miller, former U.S. senator and Georgia governor, has also expressed a preference for mandatory enrollment, saying, "If I had a choice of pre-K or 12th grade being mandatory, I'd take pre-K in a second." For many people who are convinced that preschool is a necessity, mandatory attendance becomes the next logical step. As one prominent Vermont legislator explained when he proposed a study on the cost of compulsory preschool for three- and four-year-olds, compulsion is the only way to guarantee that children have an equal opportunity for education.

Fundamentally, the preschool and kindergarten debate is not about the effectiveness or expense of the programs. At heart is the question of in whose hands the responsibility for young children should rest. On that question, plans to entrench the state further into early education cannot be squared with a free society that cherishes the primacy of the family over the state.

## Alternatives to Preschool

I've seen mothers of young children join together to create incredible early-childhood experiences. They've visited water treatment plants to see "where the poop goes" and restaurants to make and throw pizza dough. They've provided children with experiences in storytelling and hands-on museums and a study of local manatees. . . .

I've seen children wait to start preschool because their grandparents beg for more time to spend with them. These grandparents aren't teaching initial consonant sounds and letter links; they are telling stories, singing songs Mom and Dad forgot, and showing children how to bait a fish hook. Every parent must be reassured that there is no curriculum anywhere at any price that can give a child more than that.

*Karen Deerwester, "Do Kids Need Preschool?"*
South Florida Parenting, *2007, www.southflorida.com.*

## Understanding the Research

Policymakers are interested in early education for several reasons. Some proponents see preschool and kindergarten as a politically palatable way to subsidize day care. The primary argument made by Arizona policymakers, including governor Janet Napolitano, state superintendent of public instruction Tom Home, and the State School Readiness Board, is that more early learning will provide the experiences and environment necessary to promote the healthy development of children, leading to subsequent school achievement. For example,

- State superintendent of public instruction Tom Horne writes, "Studies show that a dollar spent on academically oriented all-day kindergarten can equal more than $7 or $8 spent in later grades in producing the same academic progress."

- Governor Janet Napolitano writes, "Extensive research shows that full-day kindergarten improves students' reading, writing and math skills, and it contributes to lower dropout rates."

- The State School Readiness Board writes, "Full day kindergarten can lower grade retention, improve language and math skills, lead to higher achievement test scores in eighth grade, and improve attendance and social skills."

Unfortunately, most of the research informing those statements is limited in its applicability to mainstream students and plagued by methodological shortcomings, including small sample size, high attrition rates, infrequent random selection, and infrequent use of comparison groups. Some of the research has been wholly discredited.

For instance, Superintendent Home suggests that one dollar invested in full-day kindergarten can save seven dollars in later years. Although he does not specify, this figure appears to be based on a flawed cost-benefit analysis from one study of 123 children conducted from 1962–1965, which independent peer reviewers found to be compromised by significant sampling and methodological errors. It also lacks the ability to inform the preschool discussion for mainstream children because it included only children at risk of "retarded intellectual functioning." Further undermining confidence in the results is the fact that its findings have never been replicated. . . .

## Advantages "Fade Out" over Time

Taken as a whole, a review of the research shows that some early interventions have had meaningful short-term effects on disadvantaged students' cognitive ability, grade-level retention, and special education placement. However, most research also indicates that the effects of early interventions disappear after children leave the programs.

This finding helps explain why two researchers can look at the same study and reach different conclusions: the National Center for Education Statistics (NCES) studies, for instance, which have received significant press coverage and are discussed later in detail, show a slight advantage for full-day kindergartners over half-day kindergartners as measured at the end of the kindergarten year. Critically, however, they show no differences in academic achievement between the two groups by the end of third grade. . . .

The phenomenon known as "fade out" is important to discussions of preschool and kindergarten because it means that early schooling may not measurably affect a child's later academic performance. However, if fade out occurs, not because programs are ineffective, but because the schools children later attend are unable to maintain those gains, then it is reasonable to conclude that preschool and kindergarten will not result in lasting gains unless or until elementary and secondary schools are significantly improved. Either conclusion points invariably to the need for reform within the current school system.

The few instances in which research has shown the potential of early intervention for improving children's long-term outcomes, the research has been conducted on severely disadvantaged children only in intense settings involving a level of intervention far different from either preschool or kindergarten. For instance, in the widely cited Abecedarian program, children were placed in the program as infants, at the average age of just over four months old.

Importantly, most research has concentrated on children considered to be at risk of school failure, and that research does not inform questions about the majority of mainstream students. The studies that have been conducted on mainstream children generally do not show benefits from early education programs. According to David Weikart, past president of the High/Scope Educational Research Foundation responsible for Perry Preschool, "For middle-class youngsters with a good economic basis, most programs are not able to show much in the way of difference."

## More Harm than Good

A significant body of research shows that formal early education can be detrimental to mainstream children. David Elkind, professor of child development at Tufts University and author of numerous books on cognitive and social development in children and adolescents, explains:

> The image of child competence introduced in the 1960s was intended to remedy some of the social inequalities visited upon low-income children. But the publicity given the arguments of child competence was read and heard by educators and middle-class parents as well . . . For this reason it was uncritically appropriated for middle-class children by parents and educators. While the image of childhood competence has served a useful function for low-income children and children with special needs, it has become the rationale for the miseducation of middle-class children . . .

Elkind explains that children who receive academic instruction too early—generally before age six or seven—are often put at risk for no apparent gain. By attempting to teach the wrong things at the wrong time, early instruction can permanently damage a child's self-esteem, reduce a child's natural eagerness to learn, and block a child's natural gifts and talents. He concludes:

> There is no evidence that such early instruction has lasting benefits, and considerable evidence that it can do lasting harm . . . If we do not wake up to the potential danger of these harmful practices, we may do serious damage to a large segment of the next generation . . .

The notable absence of benefits for mainstream children coupled with evidence that early education programs can be detrimental to their development should be of critical concern in light of the fact that policymakers seek preschool and full-day kindergarten for all children, not just the small percentage classified as being at risk for school failure.

*"Public subsidies offered are not enough for families below the poverty line or earning near the minimum wage."*

# Welfare Programs Help Families

## Deepak Bhargava

*Deepak Bhargava is the executive director of the Center for Community Change, an organization that helps establish and develop community organizations and focus national attention on issues related to poverty and government programs. In the following viewpoint, he asserts that working families need much more support from the government to live a "decent" life in the current economy. He recommends universal health care, more public programs and tax credits, higher minimum wages, and more job opportunity to increase the American quality of life.*

As you read, consider the following questions:

1. What percentage of American families struggles financially to maintain what the author describes as a "barebones lifestyle"?

Deepak Bhargava, "How Much Is Enough?" *The American Prospect*, vol. 15, September 2004, pp. A6–A7.

2. Why does the author use the terms "crazy quilt" and "haphazard" to describe the current collection of government programs?

3. Besides financial assistance, what other forms of public and private support would benefit families?

A dam Smith, in *The Wealth of Nations*, posed the question on how to define an adequate standard of living. "By necessaries," he wrote, "I understand not only the commodities which are indispensably necessary for support of life, but what ever the custom of the country renders it indecent for creditable people, even of the lowest order, to be without." We've been debating what's indispensable, what's indecent, and what it means to be a "creditable" person within the sphere of our common moral concern ever since.

So what does it take to live at a minimal level of decency in America today? And what is the government doing to make it happen? The answers to those questions are not heartening: It takes much more income than millions of Americans have today, and the government is not doing enough to change that. The patchwork of programs that do exist are inadequate for nearly everyone in the bottom third or bottom half of the nation's wage earners. Public subsidies offered are not enough for families below the poverty line or earning near the minimum wage, and are of little or no help to workers whose earnings get them close to a reasonable level. And for those in the middle, the benefits from these programs phase out quickly as income rises, so that additional earnings don't have much impact on disposable income. In other words, the architecture of programs that has evolved since Franklin Delano Roosevelt's famous articulation of a "freedom from want" is radically out of whack with what it costs to make it in America today.

There is broad agreement that the current federal poverty level of $18,850 for a family of four—which is less than one third of current median income for a four person family—is inadequate to meet basic needs or allow for a decent lifestyle. In fact, taking into account the true costs of goods and services, studies sponsored by Wider Opportunities for Women in states and localities around the country estimate self-sufficiency in the range of $35,000 to $50,000 per year for a family of four, about 60 percent to 75 percent of the local median income, and at least twice the current poverty threshold. Even these higher standards assume a bare-bones lifestyle: no school supplies, birthday presents, or college savings for the kids, and no savings for retirement. While 12 percent of Americans are poor under the U.S. Census Bureau's official definition of poverty, between 30 percent and 40 percent of Americans have incomes below these more realistic standards.

In other words, it's apparent that our current policies and programs are inadequate and out of date. On the labor-market side, minimum-wage standards and unemployment insurance are two of the core policies designed to help ensure the living standards of workers prior to retirement. During the past 30 years, business opposition to adequate standards has caused a substantial erosion in the adequacy of both programs. Currently, full-time, full-year work at the federal minimum wage of $5.15 an hour yields an annual income of $10,300. If the minimum wage had kept pace with inflation since the late 1960s, as it had done during the previous two decades, its current level would be more than $7.50 an hour, or $15,000 a year. What's worse, the bottom end of the labor market has returned to the Wild West conditions prevalent before the New Deal, such that enforcement of the existing wage and hour rules is disappearing. So even the paltry minimum wage we have in place is often ignored.

Meanwhile, unemployment insurance is typically limited to six months of benefits, with many eligible workers qualifying for even less. When they do receive the money, average benefits are only about 35 percent of prior wages. And because eligibility requires significant prior work history and has

## Government Helps California Families Get Ahead

Policies for the working poor are being piloted in California. These community programs don't rely on the old tools. Instead, they've worked with 5,000 families to cut an innovative deal: if you put aside savings to buy a home, go back to school or pursue some type of self-employment, we'll match your savings $2 for every $1 you put in an account. We'll help you create a budget to meet your savings goals and build your credit. And we'll help you open a bank account, IRA, and use other types of financial services.

*Anne Stuhldreher, "A New Way to Help California's Poor,"*
San Diego Union Tribune, *February 3, 2006.*

narrow qualifying rules based on the reason for loss of employment, only about 40 percent of all unemployed workers qualify for benefits.

Business has dramatically shifted responsibility and risk to workers in other ways as well. For instance, companies have sharply curtailed or eliminated workers' employer-based health coverage and defined-benefit pension plans in which the plan guarantees a specific monthly pension benefit.

Unfortunately, that leaves the poor dependent on government programs that are deeply flawed. There are a number of publicly funded programs designed to fill the gap between what people earn in the market and what they need. These programs reflect a crazy quilt of eligibility standards. For example, while children in most states are eligible for Medicaid up to about 200 percent of the federal poverty level, the income cutoff for their parents is typically much lower. Food stamps are limited to those below 130 percent, and eligibility for the Earned Income Tax Credit for two-parent families with two or more children is limited to those with incomes below

185 percent of the poverty level. Federally subsidized child-care assistance is legally available up to 85 percent of state median income, and some federal housing subsidies are available up to 80 percent of area median income, but—thanks to limited funding and red tape blocking the way of many who seek help—only a small fraction of eligible families actually get child care or housing help. If you find all of that confusing, well, that's exactly the point. This haphazard set of eligibility rules has grown up over the last 30 years, representing political compromises that don't rationally meet the needs of the low-income families they're supposed to help.

What needs to be done? On the public side, we need a combination of macroeconomic and public job-creation policies to ensure that everyone who wants to work can work. We need universal health insurance and as a step toward that, an expansion and stabilization of public programs to cover more low-income wage earners and their families. The public system of supports for workers whose incomes are below the threshold—child care, housing, refundable tax credits—needs to provide more adequate benefits to all who are eligible, and in a simpler more accessible fashion. In some cases, we need to raise eligibility standards for programs to reach struggling families not now eligible.

On the private side, we need to establish a higher set of standards for employers, who in turn need to offer a minimum wage that will provide at least a poverty-level income to a full-time, full-year worker, automatically adjusted to keep up with increased costs and productivity. The unemployment-insurance system needs to be updated so that low-wage and part-time workers become eligible, benefits are available to workers who are in school (or training programs are offered to update their skills), and benefit levels are improved. Labor-law reform (and enforcement of existing labor and discrimination laws) would restore some balance of power in the workplace and would allow workers to go beyond federal or state minimums to secure a fair share of the profits their work creates. Through a combination of employer-provided sick leave and longer-term paid family leave, the need for both the time and income to meet family needs must also be addressed. Focusing on the private sector's responsibility is important, both because budget deficits will constrain the public sector and because we don't want businesses to shift the cost of bad jobs on to the rest of us.

These changes would address the financial shortfall of so many Americans today. But money alone won't satisfy the social contract. More is needed. First, everyone who wants to work must have the opportunity to do so. Second, the right combination of work and income must be available for those who, from time to time, must interrupt their work for health reasons or family caregiving responsibilities. Third, the terms and conditions of work must be consistent with minimum standards for dignity and self-respect and bring an end to the exploitation of vulnerable immigrant workers, discrimination against people of color, and unsafe and unhealthy conditions that still mar many workplaces.

The discussion about what constitutes a decent standard of living is really a proxy for a much bigger debate between two competing sets of values. The market economy rests on a foundation of self-interest and individual risk, limited theoretically by certain rules and norms regarding transparency and fair dealing (Enron and Wal-Mart notwithstanding). A parallel set of values, arising from both secular and faith traditions, holds that we're all equal stakeholders in society, deserving of respect, dignity, and some fair share of the country's bounty. The latter tradition has been losing out badly over the past few decades.

What we need, then, are much higher standards, both in terms of income and quality of life. Broadening these standards is necessary for building a new generation of policies that is moral and just. It would also help build a coalition to achieve them: A constituency much larger than the 12 percent of Americans officially classified as poor would support such a broader definition. And a more expansive definition of what it takes to make it in America would logically force us to ask an even more provocative question: How much income (and wealth) is too much?

> "Movement away from the welfare state is movement toward better family values."

# Welfare Programs Do Not Help Families

*Vedran Vuk*

*Vedran Vuk was a 2006 Summer Fellow at the Mises Institute, a research center that supports a market economy and property rights and that believes government involvement in private affairs is economically and socially destructive. In the following viewpoint, the author criticizes the "welfare state," or a nation in which the government actively involves itself in the welfare of its people. He makes the argument that families should be responsible for taking care of themselves and that the (tax-funded) public assistance programs of a welfare state undermine the authority and cohesiveness of families.*

As you read, consider the following questions:

1. According to the author, how does the responsibility of taking care of family members promote the formation of healthy families?

Vedran Vuk, "The Welfare State's Attack on the Family," *Ludwig von Mises Institute*, July 12, 2006. Reproduced by permission.

2. Why does the author say that federal funding for single mothers increases the number of single mothers?

3. According to the author, why are the goals of government in conflict with the cohesiveness of the family?

When my brother and I were babies [in Yugoslavia], my grandparents stepped in to take care of us while my mother and father worked. My parents in turn provided for the whole household living under one roof to save money. When my father moved to the United States and made more money, he made sure that my grandparents would be taken care of.

During the Balkan War, members of my family were forcefully removed and became refugees due to the conflict. When they lost everything, guess who took care of them? The whole family together sent money and whatever supplies that they could.

So was the rule everywhere before the welfare state: your parents who took care of you financially as a child—you may need to help them in the future. This basic element of family life seems to be mind-boggling to supporters of the welfare state. Proponents of the welfare state constantly speak about our responsibility to society through redistributionist taxes.

## Who Should Care for Whom?

I have no responsibility to society as a whole, to some stranger I've never met. I personally feel that I do have a responsibility toward my immediate family. Programs like TANF (Temporary Assistance for Needy Families), Social Security, and unemployment insurance take away our responsibility to the family and place it in the hands of the state. They crowd out our sense of moral responsibility.

Family was an integral way of caring for individuals as a whole for centuries. Supporters of the welfare state forget the past.

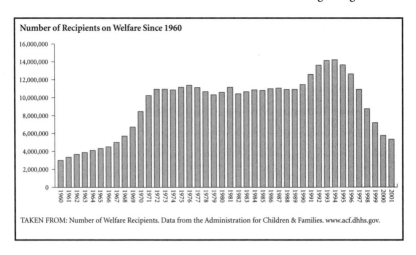

**Number of Recipients on Welfare Since 1960**

TAKEN FROM: Number of Welfare Recipients. Data from the Administration for Children & Families. www.acf.dhhs.gov.

Before the advent of Social Security, what happened to people who lived past 65 years? Did these people just starve to death from hunger by the tens of thousands? No. Did a huge wave of charitable organizations come to their rescue? Not always. So, how did they survive? Everyone can agree that there were no mass deaths of 65-year-old people recorded in the Great Depression before Social Security took effect.

These people survived under a basic principle in life. You take care of your kids, and one day, they will take care of you. In the past, having children was an investment in your future. You knew that one day your children would take care of your needs as you took care of theirs.

This created many incentives that produced a healthy family. For one thing, you had to be somewhat nicer to your children and make sure that you instilled good values. Children without a good work ethic or good values are not likely to perform well in the job market. A parent would have to teach these values to children to ensure his or her own needs at a later time. Responsibility to the family ranked highly. Without this ingrained in a child, he or she might grow up one day and never return the nurturing given by parents early in life.

## Government Involvement Encourages Bad Habits

With government attempting to smooth over every mistake in life, we get very different incentives. If your parents are entirely subsidized on welfare, how much do they really care about your future? Parents usually care for their children and want the best for them. But parents who know that they either raise their child right or don't eat in the future will try [many] times harder to make sure their child stays away from drugs, crime, and other bad decisions. . . .

It's not easy to have a child whether you are rich or poor. At any point in life a baby is difficult to raise and deal with. Even with a college degree, a young mother will have just as much difficulty as a teenager. These are facts of life. Raising children is hard work! The welfare state has reinforced the idea that if anything is hard, it must be wrong.

Doing the right thing is not easy. Difficulty does not justify immoral actions. Sure, taking care of your elderly parents is harder on you than having the state do it. But is it your moral responsibility? Yes. It is not the responsibility of some other taxpayer who does not even know your parents. Anyone who would leave it to strangers to care for their elderly parents should be ashamed.

## Destruction of the Family

Before the welfare state, there existed incentives to have children and ensure your own future. Now, we have incentives to break the family apart. TANF actually gives more money to single moms. This may seem like a great program to help single mothers in need, but in reality, the program makes it easier for the man in the family to leave. It reduces the man's practical responsibility to stay and raise the child. The program creates more single mothers! And some day, it will be the government, not his offspring, who will provide for the man who left. . . .

Unemployment insurance has also undermined society. During the Great Depression, there were great movements of people to find jobs. If there was a job somewhere, people went. Now, with unemployment and welfare people stay in the same city watching everything around them rot and decay. Government housing keeps them complacent as they beg for yet more assistance. When times get tough, people will move to get jobs. The Great Depression has already proved this. Did millions die without welfare or unemployment insurance? No. Does it improve people's lives to subsidize their staying in one place? No.

## Families Care for Each Other

I can speak from experience. I've seen charity and love within my own family overcoming all obstacles in our times. Being born in former Yugoslavia, my family was accustomed to scarcity and socialist poverty. But I saw the family working together to achieve the greater ends of each member. This was not a socialist kind of responsibility. A family member cared for you at a point in time; later you cared for them.

My father's mother spent all her savings of thirty years to send my father to medical school. There was no government help there. When, years down the road, she had to retire because of breast cancer, guess who paid her bills and medical treatments. My aunt and uncle also assisted by living with her and taking care of her on a daily basis. There was no dependable national healthcare. There was no subsidized retirement home or social security. The children she gave birth to and raised responsibly made sure that she was well taken care of until her final days. Each was fulfilling his responsibility of a child to his mother.

The agenda of the state is to break up the family. The more you depend on the state, the more you justify its existence, and the larger it grows. The idea that people can provide things for themselves either individually or through the family frightens the state. It delegitimizes its role. The role of the family is dangerous to its survival.

Movement away from the welfare state is movement toward better family values and better family cohesiveness.

The death of the family is the life of the state.

# Periodical Bibliography

*The following articles have been selected to supplement the diverse views presented in this chapter.*

Rebecca Brown Burton "A New Marriage Proposal: How a Controversial Program Promotes Matrimony as a Way to Tackle Poverty," *Time*, November 8, 2004.

*Economic Opportunity Report* , "Poor, Employed Women Suffer Loss of Insurance under Welfare Reform," April 10, 2006.

*Economist* "Tough Love Works: Welfare to Work," July 29, 2006.

Jessica Fraser "The Abraham Cherrix Cancer Story the Media Won't Print: Harry Hoxsey's Cancer Cures and the U.S. Government Campaign to Destroy Them," *News Target.com*, August 3, 2006, www.newstarget.com/01985.2html.

Robert P. George "Families and First Principles: The Conservative Fight to Protect Life and Defend Marriage," *National Review*, February 12, 2007.

Leon Kumove "A Job Is Not Enough," *Community Action*, September 25, 2006.

Sharon Lerner "The Bush Administration's Misguided Poverty Cure," *Nation*, July 5, 2004.

Jeff A. Schnepper "A 'Singular' Tax Penalty," *USA Today (Magazine)*, November 2004.

Aaron Siegel "Youth Feel the Brunt of Low Taxes," *Investment News*, February 26, 2007.

Robert Slaby, Sharon Loucks, and Patricia Stelwagon "Why Is Preschool Essential in Closing the Achievement Gap?" *Educational Leadership and Administration*, Fall 2005.

Jim Small "Arizona Lawmakers Look to Policy to Attack Rising Childhood Obesity Rates," *Arizona Capitol Times*, February 24, 2006.

Austin Webb "Regaining Our Pioneer Spirit: Staying Home and Standing Out," *Practical Homeschooling*, March–April 2006.

# For Further Discussion

## Chapter 1

1. Arlene Skolnick paints a picture of the modern family as one that looks familiar but with members who relate to each other in ways that are completely new. Jennie Bristow paints one that appears to be very divergent from traditional household and childrearing models but in which participants relate to each other much as they have throughout history. Both authors make predictions about what will happen to the institution of the family in the near and relatively near future. Which prediction do you think is most likely to be correct? List any alternative futures for the institution of the family that you believe the authors failed to address.

2. Heather Ann Gannon presents an argument for allowing same-sex marriage based on the concept of civil rights and people's basic freedom to marry whomever they love. Donald DeMarco presents an argument against same-sex marriage based on traditions from recorded history and biology, in which he acknowledges that all people are free to form relationships with those they love but claims that the obligations of marriage transcend the relationship between two people. If Gannon and DeMarco were to directly debate this topics, on what points would they be likely to agree? On what points would they be likely to disagree? Describe a possible compromise regarding the rights of same-sex couples to associate intimately that could satisfy both authors.

3. Brigitte Berger and Jennifer Roback Morse present two very different family dynamics. Berger describes a long tradition of mothers who worked to contribute to the

household income and were supported by non-parental, non-detrimental childcare. In contrast, Roback suggests one spouse should contribute to the family income so the other dedicates him- or herself (usually herself) to the tasks of maintaining the home and personally raising children, because children need their parents. Considering that families will always need economic support and children will always need rearing and guidance, do you think one strategy stands out as clearly superior to the other? Explain which strategy you would use in your own family, if you could only choose one of these two.

# Chapter 2

1. Both Debora Spar and Darlene Gerow state that a market exists to help childless couples form families by acquiring children, either through assisted reproductive technology or adoption. Both authors acknowledge that a market for babies has distasteful elements, specifically the buying and selling of human genetic elements (from sperm to children), usually with wealthier people as customers and poorer people as suppliers. Spar uses this point to argue that the market needs to be brought into the open and regulated, but Gerow uses it to argue that the market should be closed. Are the infertility treatment and adoption industries exploiting the poor for the benefit of the rich? Even if you think that such an inequity is generally unfair, should government limit the ability of rich people to acquire children simply because poor people cannot do so?

2. Anne Patterson uses compelling emotional language to support her argument that being adopted away from the natural family is harmful to the separated mother and child. Janet Albrechtsen uses straightforward language and statistical references to support her argument that children are being harmed by the reluctance of the Australian gov-

ernment to place them in permanent, stable homes for the sake of giving unfit parents too many chances to reform. Which viewpoint do you think makes the stronger case? Did the author's choice of using either emotional language or statistics (depending on which author you chose) influence your decision? Which language strategy do you consider more effective for making persuasive arguments?

3. Maxine Frith reports on research revealing that women who get pregnant in their forties face significant health risks. Mark Henderson reports on research suggesting that women having babies well into their fifties face no additional risks to their health. Both authors focus on how motherhood later in life affects the well-being of the parent, but only Henderson broaches the topic of how being born to an older mother might affect the well-being of the child. Is the age of a potential mother a legitimate topic of public debate? Should doctors worry about how the age of mothers might affect the lives of the children they help these women conceive? Or is a doctor's responsibility only to their adult female patients?

# Chapter 3

1. Martin Daly and Margot Wilson present alarming statistics from several countries that document the terrible harm some children have suffered at the hands of stepparents (and other unrelated romantic partners of their custodial parents) and link them to theories of evolution. Elizabeth Bartholet dismisses the importance of DNA and argues that genetics are not the proper basis for assessing the relationships between children and their primary caretakers. Do you think that the development of DNA testing technology, which has transformed how society assigns parentage and its accompanying obligations, has been a help or a hindrance in family law and child welfare? Does

genetic information make decisions about children's futures easier or harder to determine?

2. Author Judith Wallerstein has dedicated much of her career to studying the lasting negative impacts of divorce on children. E. Mavis Hetherington has concluded that most children of divorce recover and go on to lead normal lives. Do you think that research results showing positive outcomes of divorce will affect the divorce rate? Is a persistent national dialogue about the damage divorce can cause likely to increase divorce rates? Does an understanding of how bad divorce can be for children serve as a point of reflection and possible dissuasion for adults considering divorce?

# Chapter 4

1. Steven Nock writes that it is in government's best interest to promote the welfare of the family because family is a stabilizing force. John Fox decries such public policies as open discrimination against people who have not married or had children. Do you think family-friendly policies are unfair? Do single people personally benefit enough from living in a society filled with married couples and children to justify tolerating discriminatory practices?

2. Susanna Cooper and Kara Dukakis outline the many benefits preschool provides for children and argue that it is in the best interest of the state of California to make sure that every child attends. Darcy Olsen disputes these benefits and suggests that the preschool movement hides a government agenda to undermine parental authority. Do you think the government is solely interested in educating a population to meet the professional demands of the future? Or does government seek to take over the task of childrearing as yet another example of how it lacks faith in individual citizens to do the right thing for their fami-

lies? Extrapolating from what you have read in these two viewpoints, do you think any level of education should be mandatory?

3. Deepak Bhargava states in no uncertain terms that government needs to spend more money on programs to help working-class families attain a higher standard of living. Vedran Vuk argues that welfare programs should be abolished because they increase personal irresponsibility and erode private familial sources of support that endured throughout history. Do you think society has a responsibility to give adults money and benefits at the expense of other adults who are supporting themselves? Do you think society has a responsibility to support adults with children for the sake of the children who are necessarily dependent and cannot help themselves? Do you think individuals should have the right to refuse to pay taxes that support causes they do not value?

# Organizations to Contact

*The editors have compiled the following list of organizations concerned with the issues debated in this book. The descriptions are derived from materials provided by the organizations. All have publications or information available for interested readers. The list was compiled on the date of publication of the present volume; the information provided here may change. Be aware that many organizations take several weeks or longer to respond to inquiries, so allow as much time as possible.*

**American Coalition for Fathers and Children (ACFC)**
1718 M Street NW, #187, Washington, DC   20036
(800) 978-3237
e-mail: info@acfc.org
Web site: www.acfc.org

The ACFC dedicates its efforts to the creation of a family law system, legislative system, and public awareness that promotes equal rights for all parties affected by divorce and the breakup of a family, or establishment of paternity. Its members believe that children deserve to spend an equal amount of time with both parents, that grandparents should be guaranteed involvement, and that gender bias should be removed from family law and legislation. The organization publishes quarterly *The Liberator*, which challenges readers to critically examine the premises underlying government policy and the erosion of family integrity in society.

**Bastard Nation**
P.O. Box 1469, Edmond, OK   73083-1469
(415) 704-3166
e-mail: bn@bastards.org
Web site: www.bastards.org

The mission of Bastard Nation is to provide adoptees with complete access to state-held records, including original birth and adoption records, in the United States and Canada. The members maintain that it is a basic civil right to have all knowledge pertaining to their historic, genetic, and legal identities. It is a non-profit agency that sponsors educational programs and conducts political advocacy.

### Covenant Marriage Movement (CMM)
P.O. Box 780, Forest, VA   24551
(800) 311-1662 • fax: (434) 525-9480
e-mail: info@covenantmarriage.com
Web site: www.covenantmarriage.com

The Covenant Marriage Movement is an affiliation of religious leaders, politicians, educators, clergy, counselors, and social scientists affirming the importance of establishing and maintaining wholesome lifelong marriage relationships. They espouse the religious view of marriage as a covenant relationship over and beyond an understanding of marriage as a contractual relationship or simply an institution. Their Web site is a resource of information about legal and religious events that promote covenant marriage, and provides support for couples and congregations interested in it.

### Families and Work Institute (FWI)
267 Fifth Avenue, Floor 2, New York, NY   10016
(212) 465-2044 • fax: (212) 465-8637
Web site: www.familiesandwork.org

FWI addresses the changing nature of work and family life by fostering mutually supportive connections among workplaces, families, and communities. It publishes research reports and other information under the headings of Work-Life, Fatherhood, Families and Communities, Development of Young Children, Ask the Children, Education and Care, and Parenting.

### Focus on the Family
8605 Explorer Drive, Colorado Springs, CO   80920
(800) 232-6459 • fax: (719) 531-3424
Web site: www.family.org

Focus on the Family is a conservative Christian organization that promotes traditional family values and gender roles. *Focus on the Family*, its monthly magazine, addresses the challenges and joys of everyday life, relationships, parenting, and faith. The organization's founder, child psychologist Dr. James Dobson, makes a daily audio broadcast that can be heard online and on syndicated radio stations.

**Home School Legal Defense Association (HSLDA)**
P.O. Box 3000, Purcellville, VA   20134-9000
(540) 338-5600 • fax: (540) 338-2733
e-mail: info@hslda.org
Web site: www.hslda.org

The HSLDA is a non-profit organization established to defend and advance the constitutional right of parents to direct the education of their children and to protect family freedoms. It acts as an advocacy group in the legal system, in politics, and in the media, and funds research projects about the benefits of homeschooling. It is the parent organization of the National Center for Home Education.

**Lambda Legal**
120 Wall Street, #1500, New York, NY   10005-3904
(212) 809-8585
Web site: www.lambdalegal.org

Lambda Legal is a national organization committed to achieving full recognition of the civil rights of lesbians, gay men, bisexuals, transgender people, and those with HIV through impact litigation, education, and public policy work. Headquartered in New York City with offices in Atlanta, Chicago, Dallas, and Los Angeles, its public education and legal experts work with cases and issues that they judge will have the greatest impact on protecting and advancing the rights of lesbian, gay, bisexual, and transgendered people, and people with HIV. The organization publishes of the quarter *Lambda Legal Update*, as well as many other print and online documents and resources, in Spanish and English.

## National Council for Adoption (NCFA)
225 N. Washington Street, Alexandria, VA   22314-2561
(703) 299-6633 • fax: (703) 299-6004
e-mail: ncfa@adoptioncouncil.org
Web site: www.adoptioncouncil.org

The NCFA is a research, education, and advocacy organization whose mission is to promote the well-being of children, birthparents, and adoptive families by advocating for the positive option of adoption, for children born in the United States and abroad. The organization publishes *National Adoption Reports*, a quarterly newsletter, and of the document *Adoption Factbook*. It is also a leading source of journalist information about adoption.

## National Embryo Donation Center (NEDC)
Baptist Hospital for Women, Knoxville, TN   37934
(866) 585-8549 • fax: (865) 218-6666
Web site: www.embryodonation.org

The NEDC is a non-profit organization whose mission is to protect existence of human embryos by promoting, facilitating, and educating the public about embryo donation and adoption. It handlesthe medical, legal, and social requirements of embryo donation, and match prospective parents to genetically similar embryos—known as "snowflakes"—for implantation. As of December 2006, fifty-three babies had been born or were waiting to be born under this program.

## National Stepfamily Resource Center (NSRC)
Auburn University, Auburn, AL   36849
(334) 844-4000
e-mail: stepfamily@auburn.edu
Web site: www.stepfamilies.info

The National Stepfamily Resource Center (NSRC) is a division of Auburn University's Center for Children, Youth, and Families (CCYF). Its primary objective is serving as a clearinghouse of information, linking family science research on stepfamilies and best practices in work with couples and children in stepfamilies. Its Web site contains information about programs and services to help stepfamilies, laws and policies that affect stepfamilies, and research results as well as research participation opportunities.

**Office of Children's Issues in the Bureau of Consular Affairs**
Department of State, Office of Children's Issues, SA-29
Washington, DC   20520
(202) 736-9130 • fax: (202) 736-9080
Web site: http://travel.state.gov/family

The U.S. Department of State provides extensive information about the adoption processes in various countries and the U.S. legal requirements for bringing a child adopted abroad to the United States. The Office of Children's Issues in the Bureau of Consular Affairs hosts an informational Web site and provides brochures describing the adoption process in numerous countries.

**Society for Assisted Reproductive Technology (SART)**
1209 Montgomery Highway, Birmingham, AL   35216
(205) 978-5000 • fax: (205) 978-5015
e-mail: jzeitz@asrm.org
Web site: www.sart.org

SART promotes and advances standards for the practice of assisted reproductive technology to the benefit of patients, its members, and society at large. The organization collects data about the outcome of assisted reproductive technology (ART) procedures, creates practice guidelines and establishes minimum standards of care, serves as a watchdog organization over ART, and conducts research.

**Unmarried America**
P.O. Box 11030, Glendale, CA   91226
(818) 230-5156
e-mail: mail@unmarriedamerica.org
Web site: www.unmarriedamerica.org

Unmarried America is a nonprofit information service focusing on the interests and concerns of America's 89 million unmarried adults. Its online newspaper column provides weekly commentary about political, legal, economic, and other issues affecting unmarried people; its online library is a searchable database of information about marital status, singles' rights, family diversity, and domestic partner benefits.

## U.S. Department of Education

400 Maryland Avenue, SW, Washington, DC   20202
(800) 872-5327 • fax: (202) 401-0689
Web site: www.ed.gov

The mission of the Department of Education is to help ensure access to education for every-individual and to increase the involvement of the public, parents, and students in federal education programs. The Department of Education produces a number of newsletters, booklets, and resources that provide help for parents and teachers to strengthen the educational skills of children and update the public on educational research and innovations. The department also runs ERIC (the Education Resources Information Center), a digital library of education literature that contains more than 1.2 million documents.

# Book Bibliography

Stephen Baskerville

*Taken into Custody: The War against Fatherhood, Marriage, and the Family.* Nashville, TN: Cumberland House, 2007.

J. Kenneth Blackwell and Jerome R. Corsi

*Rebuilding America: A Prescription for Creating Strong Families, Building the Wealth of Working People, and Ending Welfare.* Nashville, TN: WND Books, 2006.

Joel D. Block and Susan Bartell

*Stepliving for Teens: Getting Along with Stepparents, Parents, and Siblings.* New York: Price Stern Sloan, 2001.

Po Bronson

*"Why Do I Love These People?": Understanding, Surviving, and Creating Your Own Family.* New York: Random House, 2006.

Elinor Burkett

*The Baby Boon: How Family-Friendly America Cheats the Childless.* New York: The Free Press, 2000.

Janet M. Currie

*The Invisible Safety Net: Protecting the Nation's Poor Children and Families.* Princeton, NJ: Princeton University Press, 2006.

Bella DePaulo

*Singled Out: How Singles Are Stereotyped, Stigmatized, and Ignored, and Still Live Happily Ever After.* New York: St. Martin's Press, 2006.

Mickey Duxbury    *Making Room in Our Hearts: Keeping Family Ties through Open Adoption.* New York: Routledge, 2006.

Kathryn Edin and *Promises I Can Keep: Why Poor* Maria Kefalas    *Women Put Motherhood before Marriage.* Berkeley: University of California Press, 2007.

Diane Ehrensaft    *Mommies, Daddies, Donors, Surrogates: Answering Tough Questions and Building Strong Families.* New York: Guilford Press, 2005.

Lawrence M.    *Private Lives: Families, Individuals,* Friedman    *and the Law.* Cambridge, MA: Harvard University Press, 2005.

Al Gore and    *Joined at the Heart: The Transforma-* Tipper Gore    *tion of the American Family.* New York: Holt, 2002.

John Harvey and *Children of Divorce: Stories of Loss* Mark Fine    *and Growth.* Mahwah, NJ: Erlbaum, 2004.

Rosanna Hertz    *Single by Chance, Mothers by Choice: How Women Are Choosing Parenthood without Marriage and Creating the New American Family.* New York: Oxford University Press, 2006.

Betty Holcomb    *Not Guilty! The Good News for Working Mothers.* New York: Touchstone Books, 2002.

Thomas A.    *Restoring the American Dream: A* Kochan    *Working Family's Agenda for America.* Cambridge, MA: MIT Press, 2006

Elizabeth Marquardt — *Between Two Worlds: The Inner Lives of Children of Divorce.* New York: Three Rivers Press, 2006.

Joel Miller — *Size Matters: How Big Government Puts the Squeeze on America's Families, Finances, and Freedom.* Nashville, TN: Thomas Nelson, 2006.

Liza Mundy — *Everything Conceivable: How Assisted Reproduction Is Changing Men, Women, and the World.* New York: Knopf, 2007.

Doreen Nagle — *But I Don't* Feel *Too Old to Be a Mommy! The Complete Sourcebook for Starting (and Re-Starting) Motherhood Beyond 35 and after 40.* Deerfield Beach, FL: Health Communications, 2002.

Anne O'Connor — *The Truth about Stepfamilies: Real American Stepfamilies Speak Out.* New York: Marlowe, 2003.

Joyce Maguire Pavao — *The Family of Adoption* Rev. Ed. Boston: Beacon Press, 2005.

Jonathan Rauch — *Gay Marriage: Why It's Good for Gays, Good for Straights, and Good for America.* New York: Holt, 2004.

Jennifer A. Reich — *Fixing the Family: Parents, Power, and the Child Welfare System.* New York: Routledge, 2005.

| Brian C. Robertson | *Day Care Deception: What the Child Care Establishment Isn't Telling Us.* San Francisco: Encounter Books, 2003. |
| --- | --- |
| Lee M. Silver | *Remaking Eden: How Genetic Engineering and Cloning Will Transform the American Family.* New York: Harper Perennial, 2007. |
| Rita James Simon and Rhonda M. Roorda | *In Their Own Voices: Transracial Adoptees Tell Their Stories.* New York: Columbia University Press, 2000. |
| Glenn T. Stanton and Bill Maier | *Marriage on Trial: The Case against Same-Sex Marriage and Parenting.* Downers Grove, IL: Intervarsity Press, 2004. |
| Leslie Morgan Steiner | *Mommy Wars: Stay-at-Home and Career Moms Face Off on Their Choices, Their Lives, Their Families.* New York: Random House, 2006. |
| Elizabeth Warren and Amelia Warren Tyagi | *The Two-Income Trap: Why Middle-Class Mothers and Fathers Are Going Broke.* New York: Basic Books, 2003. |
| Sherry A. Wells | *Warm and Wonderful Stepmothers of Famous People.* Royal Oak, MI: Lawells Publishing, 2004. |
| James Q. Wilson | *The Marriage Problem: How Our Culture Has Weakened Families.* New York: HarperCollins, 2002. |

# Index

## A

Adoptees
  abused/neglected children, 99
  anecdote by 15 year old, 101
  forced identity shift by, 91–92
  impact of lies on, 92–93
  loss of trust of, 90–91
  parental rights vs. child's welfare, 98
  self-esteem/happiness issues, 92, 100
  separation grief of, 89–91
  *See also* "A Child's Letter to Her Birth Mother"; Search Institute of Minneapolis, adoptee study
Adoption, 68, 70, 72
  adoption law, 133–134
  adoption reforms, 103–104
  arguments for promotion of, 93–94
  breakdown rates (UK), 103
  competition for infants, 81–82
  Dawkin's negative view, 133–134
  negatives aspects of, 88–95
  opposition to, in UK, 99
  parental choice for, 89
  positive aspects of, 96–104
  problems with existing system, 98–99
  successful outcomes, 99–102
  vulnerability of poor women to, 83
  *See also* Babies; Baby market; Catholic Human Services, Inc.; Concerned United Birthparents, Inc.; Heart Words: an Adoptee Advocacy and Counseling Center; North American Council on Adoptable Children
*Adoption-A New Approach* (UK White Paper), 103
*Adoption and the Care of Children-The British and American Experience* (Morgan), 99
Adoption industry
  business model, 80–81
  child relinquishment promotion, 85
  economics of, 79–80, 81
  legislative issues, 85–86
  professional marketing, 86–87
  *See also* Baby market
*The Adoption Triangle* (Pannor), 83
Adults
  impact of divorce on, 140–142, 144
  nonresolution of inner conflict in, 142–143
  suffering of, as children of divorce, 143–144
  *See also* Parents
Albrechsten, Jane, 96–104
Ambivalence, towards family success, 30
American Society for Reproductive Medicine, 110, 113
Ancestral genotypes, 121
Arizona, trend towards government preschool/kindergarten programs, 180–183
Artificial insemination, 30, 160
Ashkenazi women. *See* Jewish women, fertility study
Assisted pregnancy, 74